Refreshing and wise, *Resilient Faith* takes the words of Jesus' Sermon on the Mount right out of the "nice-but-unrealistic" box we've placed them into, and centers this rich teaching smack into our messy real lives where it belo … practical, and challenging—I loved it.

Sarah Bessey, author of *Jesus Feminis…*

Beautifully written, deeply inspiring medita… ning disciple and the senior saint—and ever… prodding, challenging, and nurturing.

Ronald J. Sider, author of *Rich Chr…* Distinguished Professor of Theology, Holistic Ministry, and … Seminary at Eastern University

When a heart is teachable in and through the trials of life, God grows a reservoir of wisdom through which he can move, act, and reveal. Sheridan Voysey is that heart and he shares much truth and wisdom in this book. Thank you, Sheridan, for leading us to deeper waters of truth in Christ.

Denalyn Lucado, coauthor with Max Lucado of *Lucado Treasury of Bedtime Prayers*

Many books have been written on the Sermon on the Mount, but few have focused on its underlying theme of resilience. Through compelling stories and deep biblical reflection, *Resilient Faith* reveals how Jesus' teaching can build spiritual, emotional, and relational strength when put into practice. I highly recommend this fine book.

Arch Hart, author of *Thrilled to Death*, and Senior Professor of Psychology and Dean Emeritus, Graduate School of Psychology, Fuller Theological Seminary

This is a wonderful collection of short but deep reflections on what a difference Jesus' Sermon on the Mount might make to us if only we let it. Read it at your own risk. Once you have read it your life may never be the same again.

Paula R. Gooder, Theologian in Residence, Bible Society, United Kingdom

When it comes to the Sermon on the Mount, Sheridan Voysey has now written the resource of first resort. What a gem!

Leonard Sweet, weekly contributor to preachthestory.com, author of *From Tablet to Table*, and professor at Drew University, George Fox University, and Tabor College

This is a powerfully written, spiritually nourishing, and practically enabling series of meditations by a master communicator, intimate with God and connected to today's culture. Here both seeker and saint will find food for the journey.

Simon Ponsonby, author of *More* and *God Is for Us*, and Pastor of Theology at St. Aldate's, Oxford

"So come . . . whoever you are. Jesus takes all." *Resilient Faith*'s first entry grabbed me and invited me to keep reading. In digestible helpings, Sheridan Voysey serves up a bold invitation to a Jesus-shaped life that woos me to say yes . . . and to keep saying yes.

Elisa Morgan, author of *The Beauty of Broken* and President Emerita, MOPS International

Sheridan's meditations on Christ's teachings are a welcome addition for anyone wanting to get caught up in this wonderful business of putting Jesus' words into practice.

Jarrod McKenna, national director of CommonGrace.org.au, cofounder of First Home Project and #LoveMakesAWay, activist, and pastor

Insightful and packed with teaching and stories that challenge and inspire us to live differently, *Resilient Faith* takes us on a beautiful journey through the Sermon on the Mount.

Patrick Regan OBE, founder and CEO of XLP, London

Sheridan is on to something here. Immersing yourself in Jesus' Sermon on the Mount will take you straight to the heart of God—and we desperately need this. You will not regret time spent in these pages!

Rob Peabody, author of *Citizen*, and director of Awaken Movement

These attractive reflections are compassionate, personal, view-altering, and priority-shaking. Sheridan Voysey is warm and sage, but unafraid to call you out. We are all benefitting from the work Jesus' Sermon has done on him!

Greg Clarke, CEO, Bible Society Australia

Here's an invitation not to be missed: to join Sheridan on that mountainside in Galilee, to hear again the words of Jesus, to see what life looks like in the kingdom of God. The view is exhilarating! It's challenging, to be sure, and risky too, but full of promise and hope.

Antony Billington, Head of Theology, London Institute for Contemporary Christianity

The crowd who climbed that day to hear Jesus preach was not just blessed with a mountaintop vista, but a view into the very heart of God's message of love. Anyone who has climbed a mountain knows the importance of a good guide, and in *Resilient Faith* Sheridan Voysey, with wisdom and clarity, guides the reader to the heights of Jesus' teaching and invites us to drink in the glorious view.

Mark Sayers, author of *Facing Leviathan* and *The Road Trip that Changed the World*, and pastor of Red Church, Melbourne, Australia

Sheridan Voysey has captured the essence of what Jesus said to the poor, the brokenhearted—and his words echo across time and into every willing heart. May you be comforted and happy as you sit and listen to the one who loved you most.

Chris Fabry, author of *Every Waking Moment*, and host of *Chris Fabry Live!*

From a personal journey through the Sermon on the Mount, Sheridan Voysey encourages disciples of Jesus to develop a strong spiritual heart. The book will prove a blessing to all, as it certainly is for me.

Rev. Keith V. Garner, Superintendent/CEO of Wesley Mission, Sydney, Australia

Resilient Faith is a compelling invitation to a life-transforming relationship with Jesus that is beyond mere belief or religion. Through insightful reflections on the Sermon on the Mount, Sheridan Voysey draws us into a living spirituality that is refreshing, restorative, relevant, radical—and all about Jesus.

Ron Nikkel, President Emeritus, Prison Fellowship International

resilient *faith*

90 MEDITATIONS ON THE LIFE-CHANGING POWER OF THE SERMON ON THE MOUNT

Sheridan Voysey

Our Daily Bread Publishing™

Resilient Faith: 90 Meditations on the Life-Changing Power of the Sermon on the Mount

Previously published as *Resilient* (Discovery House, 2015).

An Our Daily Bread Ministries Exclusive Edition

Printed in the United Kingdom

22 23 24 25 26 27 28 / 7 6 5 4 3 2

CONTENTS

PART 3: YOUR RELATIONSHIPS

PART 4: YOUR PRACTICES

PART 5: YOUR CHOICES

PART 6: YOUR RESILIENT LIFE

INTRODUCTION

My experiment began shortly after I arrived in England. Merryn and I had moved here from Australia after one of the most tumultuous experiences in our lives. After ten years of waiting, our dream of having a child had come to an abrupt end and we had made the move around the world to start our lives again. For me, the relocation meant leaving a fulfilling career in broadcasting, and for the first time in years I no longer knew who I was or why I was here. Looking back now, I see the time was perfect for the experiment.

I had read Jesus' Sermon on the Mount plenty of times before, but normally briskly. These famous words in chapters 5 to 7 of Matthew's biography of Jesus contain much reassurance—like how the grieving will be comforted, the poor blessed, and all of us provisioned by God's care. But for the most part the Sermon is challenging, demanding, radical. It was easy to breeze past the hard parts about loving one's enemies when just ahead lay the nice ones about God giving us good gifts.

Then one day I started my experiment. I decided to read the Sermon every day for a month. All of it, not just the comforting bits. Each morning I read it slowly and prayerfully, either in whole or in part, and on weekends I studied it in depth. The experiment stretched beyond one month to two, and then on to three. Before I knew it, the Sermon had taken hold of me.

And for good reason. In the Sermon I found a guide to the essential aspects of life—our callings, relationships, practices, choices. From sex to prayer to conflict to possessions, the Sermon covers the grittiest of topics without embarrassment or apology. In it I discovered the radical idea that "little people" like us are God's change agents in the world. And in it I read that if we put Jesus' words into practice we will lead resilient lives—lives that bound back after difficulty.

For most of us in the West, life is full of freedom and opportunity. We can pursue almost any career. We can live almost any lifestyle.

But dark clouds are never far away. A spouse leaves us. A client sues. Unemployment strikes us. Our dreams fail to come true. An illness, a loss, a betrayal, a tragedy—through them we find we're vulnerable to life's storms. And not only storms from without, but storms within: desires turned lustful, ambition turned idolatrous, anger turned deadly, and other sins that can drown us. In the Sermon we find One who calms storms with a word and leads us forth in strength. Though the rain comes in torrents and the floodwaters rise and the winds beat against us, we will stand, not collapse (Matthew 7:25).

My reading of the Sermon each day began to shape me—revising my priorities, keeping desires in check, putting my dreams into perspective, influencing how I should act. In living out the Sermon, I failed as much as I made progress, and still do. But because perfection isn't possible, perfection wasn't the point. My heart was slowly being recalibrated to the heart of Jesus, who lived out everything he preached. Without my realizing it, this was all helping me to start again.

I made a lot of discoveries from my experiment. Those discoveries were recorded in my journal, later written into articles for the *Our Daily Journey* devotional, and now with significant expansion and additional material, are presented in this book of ninety readings. As you'll see, while the Sermon is the main river we'll travel down, some connected streams are worth diverting into. Jesus' Sermon is expansive, drawing many biblical themes together. My advice is to read these pages slowly and prayerfully. There's no need to hurry. Resilient lives are built on a foundation, and foundations take time to prepare.

The famous words of Jesus' Sermon have been quoted by presidents, chanted by activists, pondered by theologians, and shouted by rock stars. They've been printed on posters, T-shirts, fridge magnets, and bumper stickers, depicted in artwork, shared on the net, etched in stone, and tattooed on skin. They've been admired, ignored, scorned, adored, preached, painted, and performed. But one thing is required if they're to manifest a resilient life: according to Jesus, they must be lived (Matthew 7:26–27). As you read and pray, expect to act. Expect to birth experiments in your own life.

Some days we wake to a world of crystal skies and bright possibilities. And other days it's to rain pelting our windows, thunder rattling our roofs, winds shaking our walls, and torrents threatening to overwhelm us. Jesus never said we'd be spared the storms of life. We will creak under their winds, we will be tested and stretched. But in living out Jesus' words we're told we won't break. We will recover, spring back. Just like the One who came bounding back after being stretched beyond all limits:

Scarred, but triumphant.

And ever resilient.

The famous words of

Jesus' Sermon

have been **QUOTED** by presidents, **CHANTED** by activists, **PONDERED** by theologians, and **SHOUTED** by rock stars. They've been printed on posters, T-shirts, fridge magnets, and bumper stickers, depicted in artwork, shared on the net, **ETCHED IN STONE**, and tattooed on skin. They've been **ADMIRED**, ignored, **SCORNED**, adored, **PREACHED**, painted, and **PERFORMED**. But one thing is required if they're to manifest a resilient life: according to Jesus,

they must be lived.

PART 1

Your Invitation

Yet, in the gloom a light glimmers and glows. We have received an invitation. We are invited to make a pilgrimage—into the heart and life of God.

DALLAS WILLARD[1]

One day as he saw the crowds gathering, Jesus went up on the mountainside and sat down. His disciples gathered around him, and he began to teach them.

"God blesses those who are poor and realize their need for him,
for the Kingdom of Heaven is theirs.
God blesses those who mourn,
for they will be comforted.
God blesses those who are humble,
for they will inherit the whole earth.
God blesses those who hunger and thirst for justice,
for they will be satisfied.
God blesses those who are merciful,
for they will be shown mercy.
God blesses those whose hearts are pure,
for they will see God.
God blesses those who work for peace,
for they will be called the children of God.
God blesses those who are persecuted for doing right,
for the Kingdom of Heaven is theirs.

"God blesses you when people mock you and persecute you and lie about you and say all sorts of evil things against you because you are my followers. Be happy about it! Be very glad! For a great reward awaits you in heaven. And remember, the ancient prophets were persecuted in the same way." *Matthew 5:1–12*

COME, WHOEVER YOU ARE

"God blesses those who mourn,
for they will be comforted.
God blesses those who are humble,
for they will inherit the whole earth."

MATTHEW 5:4–5

They gather on the lush, rolling slopes to hear him. He sits down, taking the customary position of a teacher, and looks as many of them in the eye as he can. He has so many things to tell them. A deep draw of breath, and then he begins to talk. "God blesses those who are poor and realize their need for him," he says, "for the Kingdom of Heaven is theirs. . . ."

If you're anything like me, you've probably read the Sermon on the Mount's "God blesses" statements—called the Beatitudes—as a list of virtues Jesus wants us to pursue. So, we think he wants us to be humble (Matthew 5:5), to hunger for justice (5:6), to be merciful (5:7), pure (5:8), and peace-loving (5:9). These are all wonderful qualities to have and are reinforced elsewhere in scripture. And given that Jesus' Sermon is all about action, it's a natural way to read these verses.

However, if we're to be consistent in reading the Beatitudes this way, some of these "virtues" become tricky. Does Jesus really want us to become poor (5:3), to mourn (5:4), or to be persecuted and insulted (5:10–11)? This way of reading the Beatitudes can also lead to a works-based understanding of God's salvation: only when we are humble, gentle, merciful, and so on, will God then "bless" us.

Perhaps Jesus was making a different point. Luke's recording of the Beatitudes suggests Jesus wasn't addressing people who *thought* they were poor, hungry, or sad, but people who literally were (Luke 6:17–23). This has led scholars like Dallas Willard, Scot McKnight, and others to suggest that Jesus' Beatitudes are not a list of virtues at all but a list of outcasts rejected by society yet blessed by Jesus.[2]

Those who assembled on the mountain to hear Jesus speak were a motley group indeed: not the happy and successful people of the world, but those who had experienced trials and trouble (Matthew 4:23–25). It was this group of people, those gathered before him, that he blessed: the economically and spiritually impoverished (5:3), the grief-stricken (5:4), the lowly (5:5), those seeking but denied justice (5:6), those who have shown mercy and lived rightly (5:7–8), peacemakers instead of political radicals (5:9), those persecuted for doing right or for following Jesus (5:10–11). All such people were "written off" by both the secular society and the religious elite of Jesus' day. To worldly leaders who valued strength rather than humility, and compliance to their wishes rather than rebellion for the sake of God, people with these qualities held little value. But they were valuable to Jesus.

If this is what Jesus is saying it means his Sermon begins with a radical idea. It means Jesus ignores the world's popularity lists. It means he welcomes all who society rejects. The doors to his kingdom are flung open to the sick, the sad, the uneducated, and un-pretty; to the picked on, the beaten up, the socially awkward, and homeless; to pushers, dealers, con artists, killers; to the addicted, or emotionally unstable; to you and to me.

So come, whoever you are.

Jesus takes us all.

The LORD is close to all who call on him,
yes, to all who call on him in truth.

PSALM 145:18

What "written off" person do you know?

How can you be as grace-full towards them as Jesus is?

COME, RICH OR POOR

They were terrified, but the angel reassured them. "Don't be afraid!" he said. "I bring you good news that will bring great joy to all people."

LUKE 2:9–10

Good news for *all* people. That's what the angel said. This radical invitation, the idea of God's house being open to all, that we are beckoned to enter it whatever state we're in, begins well before Jesus sits to give his Sermon. And while society's outcasts are given a special welcome, they're not the only ones offered the invitation.

Scene one: a small peasant home in Bethlehem, Judea.[3] There a group of shepherds kneels before a baby sleeping in a feeding trough (Luke 2:8–20). The society of the day despises these shepherds as unclean, and that is why they can't believe they're here. How could *they* have been given such a privilege?

Scene two: also in that little peasant home. Now a group of Persian princes stands gazing at that child (Matthew 2:1–12). They are powerful, esteemed, and rich—you don't bring gifts of gold, incense, and myrrh without money. Their fine clothes and jewels look out of place in this village, but soon they also kneel before this exceptional child.

For this child would become a boy and this boy a man; and this man would be found to be so much more. A carpenter by trade but a King by birth. The God of the universe visiting his people in person (John 1:1).

From the beginning this King would be different than others. As those shepherds kneel down we see he's a King for the poor, and as those princes kneel down we see he's a King for the rich. A fisherman kneels down—here's a King for the workers (Luke 5:8); a government official seeks his help—here's a King for the rulers (John 4:46). And what kind of King hobnobs with both religious leaders *and* sinners (Luke 7:36–38)?

This kind of King.

Jesus begins his Sermon on the Mount lifting up the "have nots"—the lowly, the poor, the ridiculed and unwanted—making it clear that while society might reject them, he does not. But that doesn't mean Jesus is automatically against the "haves." Rich or poor, ruler or worker, priest or sinner, he came for us all. We can be wealthy or destitute, powerful or lowly; we can be burdened with all the shame our sins have brought upon us. Yet this King will accept us, heal us, forgive us, change us.

Kneeling is most fitting before a King born for all.

> Therefore, God elevated him to the place of highest honor
> and gave him the name above all other names,
> that at the name of Jesus every knee should bow,
> in heaven and on earth and under the earth,
> and every tongue declare that Jesus Christ is Lord,
> to the glory of God the Father.
>
> PHILIPPIANS 2:9–11

Have you ever felt unworthy of meeting Jesus?
Have you ever thought others unworthy of him too?

COME AND BE FORGIVEN

By this time it was about noon, and darkness fell across the whole land until three o'clock.

LUKE 23:44

Things start well enough as Jesus begins his mission. Crowds flock to him, amazed at his miracles, and the doors of every synagogue are open to his teaching. Jesus is on the speaking circuit and is as popular as any itinerant preacher could wish to be. But public sentiment will change.

The religious leaders will be the first to raise alarm, suspicious of the company he'll keep (Mark 2:16), the claims he'll make (14:61–64), and the power he'll heal by (3:22). His neighborhood will ignore him (6:3), his synagogue will drive him out of town (Luke 4:29), and even his family will feel embarrassed by his actions (Mark 3:21). By the end of his days he'll have been betrayed by a colleague, disowned by a friend, deserted by his followers, cursed by a thief, and seemingly abandoned by God himself. During his final hour he will be enveloped in darkness—cold, naked, exposed, and oh, so alone.

The crowd's praise will fall silent, the loyalty of his followers will prove shallow, curses will be hurled, nails will be hammered, crosses will be raised, and all those he's fed, befriended, healed, and forgiven will be nowhere to be seen. All he'll hear are the snickers of his betrayers, the whimpers of his mother, and the murmurs of the soldiers who gamble for his garments.

This "political disturber" will be quashed.

This "blasphemous healer" will be silenced.

The sky will turn dark. A tear will fall from heaven.

And at that moment, all our sins will be forgiven.

We must remember all this as we read the Sermon on the Mount. As Jesus preaches on that hillside he knows what's ahead—that most of those listening so eagerly to him will soon deny him. The people he blesses in the Beatitudes will end up cursing him in their rejection. Those he came to be with will leave him dying alone.

That most likely includes me, had I been there, and probably you too. And that makes his death for us so much more astounding. Jesus invites us into his kingdom, and we abandon him. And then he offers to forgive us.

Come and be forgiven.

"Friends, I realize that what you and your leaders did to Jesus was done in ignorance. But God was fulfilling what all the prophets had foretold about the Messiah—that he must suffer these things. Now repent of your sins and turn to God, so that your sins may be wiped away."

ACTS 3:17–19

Picture yourself at Jesus' crucifixion.
Where are you in the crowd and what are you saying?
Picture Jesus looking at you from the cross.
How does he look and what is he saying to you?

COME AND BE RESTORED

So all of us who have had that veil removed can see and reflect the glory of the Lord. And the Lord—who is the Spirit—makes us more and more like him as we are changed into his glorious image.

2 CORINTHIANS 3:18

I've had the privilege of interviewing many fascinating people during my years as a radio host. Ken Cooper's story is one I won't forget.

By all impressions, Ken was the kind of guy you'd want living next door: a loving husband and father, a respected community leader, and a role model for underprivileged children. But this mild-mannered neighbor had a dark side—Ken moonlighted as one of Florida's most wanted criminals.

Ken began shoplifting as a child, was stealing cars by the time he reached college, and turned to robbing banks when his wife died early from cancer. "My robberies had nothing to do with money," he told me. "The purpose was to feel alive—to defy this dead, depressed state I was in from losing my wife."

Ken's thirteen-year double life ended when he was shot during a bank robbery and sentenced to ninety-nine years in The Rock, Florida's infamous prison. With just five guards controlling nine hundred inmates, The Rock was a hellhole of knifings, beatings, murders, and rape. But while there, Ken heard about Jesus from a prison chaplain and soon became a Christian. Some of Ken's cell mates did too. And their lives began to change.

One day Ken and his friends adopted a kitten, who they named Mr. Magoo. Mr. Magoo's back had been broken for fun by other inmates, and he was blind from acid they'd thrown in his face. Ken and his friends held Mr. Magoo each day, took turns feeding him, even prayed for his sight to return. Mr. Magoo was lavished with love. And his sight did return! Other miracles began to happen too. Rape rates began to decrease at The Rock and prison guards began asking Ken and his fellow Christians for prayer. But perhaps nothing signifies the change in the prisoners' lives better than their kind treatment of Mr. Magoo.

The justice system could sentence Ken and his cell mates for their behavior but it couldn't change their desires. As the apostle Paul says, while civil and religious laws are good and have their place, they can only help restrain evil at best, or at worst condemn us when we break them (Romans 7:7–12; 13:1–5). Laws can't change our hearts.

In contrast Jesus, by his Spirit, offers inner change. He doesn't just forgive us, he transforms us—restoring our souls to make us "more and more like him as we are changed into his glorious image" (2 Corinthians 3:18). Jesus restores the image of God in us that got distorted through sin, making us people of love, joy, peace, patience, kindness, goodness, faithfulness, gentleness, and self-control instead (Galatians 5:22–23).

Jesus will have a lot to say about ethical living as his Sermon continues. We'll come to grief trying to live out his instructions unless we realize he's there to empower us from within. On this Ken Cooper would concur.

For here is the invitation that turns hardened criminals into kitten-protecting gentlemen.

Instead, let the Spirit renew your thoughts and attitudes. Put on your new nature, created to be like God—truly righteous and holy.

EPHESIANS 4:23–24

Are you focusing on "being good" rather than letting Jesus change you?

What sin or weakness will you offer to Jesus today, to have transformed into his character?

COME TO BE KNOWN

You know when I sit down or stand up.
You know my thoughts even when I'm far away.

PSALM 139:2

He knows you. He knows every detail and nanosecond of your existence—every atom, molecule, skin cell, and ligament; every hope, dream, interest, and achievement; every strength, weakness, gladness, and grief. He knows you intimately, through and through.

He knows every movement you will make today (Psalm 139:2–3)—every action, step, and pause for rest; every blink, glance, and breath. He knows when I will stop typing this paragraph, and when you will stop reading it. He knows everything about you, and he knows it thoroughly.

He knows every thought you will have today—every joy, question, doubt, and concern. Like a long-married husband who knows his wife so well he can finish her sentences, God knows the next word you'll say before it's left your lips (139:4).

He knows you, he's familiar with you—he knows your complete personality. He knows your emotional triggers, behavioral patterns, your bad habits and comfort zones. He knows what you're good at, lousy at, tempted by, and victorious over. He can unravel the intricate workings of your heart when you remain confused.

There is no rock large enough, no place far enough, no darkness thick enough to hide you from him (139:7–12). But why would you hide? Loneliness isn't just the feeling of being alone, but of being surrounded by many and known by none. But he knows you. He's the knowing One.

He was there as you were crafted in the womb (139:13–15). He remembers the headlines from the day of your birth, and knows the events to take place on your final day on earth (139:16). He knows what your future holds, and the pathways you will take to arrive there. He knows you.

In a world of global connections but ever-declining intimacy, of burgeoning cities with more and more alienated souls, of billions of individuals who secretly wonder if anyone really cares, here is a truth that heals and liberates:

The One who invites you on that hillside knows you.

He knows you through and through.

"And the very hairs on your head are all numbered."

MATTHEW 10:30

How does it feel to be known so intimately?

In return, how intimately would you say you know God right now?

HE KNOWS YOU.

He knows every detail and

nanosecond of your existence—

EVERY ATOM, molecule,

skin cell, and ligament;

EVERY HOPE, DREAM,

interest, and achievement;

EVERY STRENGTH, weakness,

GLADNESS, and grief.

HE KNOWS YOU intimately,

through and through.

COME TO BE EMBRACED

Jesus replied, "All who love me will do what I say.
My Father will love them, and we will come
and make our home with each of them."

JOHN 14:23

As a toddler, Adrian Edwards was separated from his parents. Shunted between institutions and foster homes for most of his life, he drifted into crime young. As a teenager he was convicted of armed robbery and spent time in Western Australia's Fremantle Jail. There, in a strange twist of fate, he met his father—who was serving time for murder. Adrian was released, but longed to see his father again.

And he did, when he was convicted a second time. Adrian served his sentence and was again released. But his father-hunger remained.

Finally, Adrian committed a string of armed robberies which brought him back into the courts, where an extended sentence was given. "Adrian is looking forward to spending a long period of time incarcerated with his father," his lawyer informed the judge. Adrian's plan to be with his dad was finally fulfilled.

Orphans forever long for their parents' embrace and can go to extraordinary lengths to replace it. Thankfully there is a God who longs for his children even more, who goes to extraordinary lengths to embrace *them*.

"I will not abandon you as orphans," Jesus told his disciples (John 14:18). They had met their Maker-incarnate and would soon lose him for a time, but they were not to fret. He was going to prepare a heavenly room for them and return to collect them (14:3). He was sending them his Spirit, "who will never leave you" (14:16). And as the Spirit was received into the disciples' hearts, Jesus said something extraordinary would happen: Father, Son, and Spirit together would come and live within them (14:23). The disciples would be wrapped in the embrace of God, in warmth, in welcome.

When Jesus sits on that mountain giving his Sermon, inviting us to follow, he doesn't just invite us into a new philosophy, lifestyle, or social group. He invites us into the very life of God—where Father, Son, and Spirit embrace as one. "I am in my Father, and you are in me, and I am in you," he says (John 14:20). The implications are astounding. We are in God's heart and he is in ours.

What an invitation for Adrian Edwards, and the rest of us.

Love the Son, receive the Spirit, and be embraced in the arms of God.

> I pray that from his glorious, unlimited resources he will empower you with inner strength through his Spirit. Then Christ will make his home in your hearts as you trust in him. Your roots will grow down into God's love and keep you strong.
>
> EPHESIANS 3:16–17

When you feel most abandoned are you ever really alone? How can God's embrace help make you resilient today?

COME TO BE REWARDED

"God blesses you when people mock you and persecute you and lie about you and say all sorts of evil things against you because you are my followers. Be happy about it! Be very glad! For a great reward awaits you in heaven."

MATTHEW 5:11–12

Janice is an attractive woman in her mid-thirties. She has looks, friends, and a successful career. A few years ago she also became a Christian—to the horror of her atheist father. Since then, visits home have become more and more difficult. Each week her father pummels her with reasons why she should abandon her "fairy tale" faith.

There is a kind of concern behind the father's relentless pursuit of Janice's de-conversion. Janice longs to be married but has decided to marry only a Christian. Her father wants to see his daughter fulfilled and sees her faith as the roadblock. "What you believe is a lie," he tells her, "and it's keeping you from marrying available men." Janice often feels weary enduring her father's words.

Jesus tells us following him can result in trouble (Matthew 5:10–12). Almost all of his apostles will meet a violent death, and a myriad of Christians throughout the centuries will lose their lives following him too. Most of us won't face that kind of persecution. For us the trials may come in the form of ridicule, lost job opportunities or, like Janice, family tension. Jesus foresees his coming will divide whole households along borderlines of belief. "Your enemies will be right in your own household!" he says (10:36). Ironically, following the Prince of Peace can result in war.

But Jesus also says those who suffer for his name will be rewarded. The poor will receive the kingdom, the humble will inherit the earth, those hungry for justice will be satisfied, the pure in heart will see God. God himself is the ultimate prize, as is his kingdom (5:12), but Jesus also promises rewards in this life too, like relationships to match our sacrifice (Luke 18:29–30). Whatever the rewards are and whenever they come, we don't serve a God who demands obedience for the sake of it. This God loves to reward us.

I admire my friend Janice. To follow Jesus, she has faced the full force of family opposition to her faith and denied her own desires. She loves her parents, continually weathering their attacks on her beliefs. And as her older sister has a child, her younger sister gets married, and her own wait for a single Christian man stretches on, Janice stays faithful to her first love.

One day she will receive her reward in full.

> Peter said, "We've left our homes to follow you."
> "Yes," Jesus replied, "and I assure you that everyone who has given up house or wife or brothers or parents or children, for the sake of the Kingdom of God, will be repaid many times over in this life, and will have eternal life in the world to come."
>
> LUKE 18:28–30

Has your obedience to Jesus ever caused you to suffer?
Is he a higher priority than your desires?

COME TO EXPAND YOUR HEART

"God blesses those who hunger and thirst for justice,
for they will be satisfied."

MATTHEW 5:6

Dallas Willard once described the Sermon on the Mount as a pilgrimage into the heart and life of God.[4] I think he was right. And as we journey into the Sermon, we shouldn't be surprised to find our own hearts expanding as Jesus shows us what is of greatest concern to God.

We've already established the Beatitudes aren't a list of character traits we should be aiming for. Jesus isn't inviting us to become poor, to mourn, or get persecuted so we can be "blessed." The Beatitudes are a list of people particularly on God's heart.

Read through scripture and it soon becomes apparent God has always had a particular concern for the poor, the forgotten, and the vulnerable (Deuteronomy 10:18; 15:11). When God arrives on earth in human form, these are the very people he blesses first. And so here's the key question: Shouldn't the people on God's heart be the people on our hearts too?

If God blesses the poor, shouldn't we too? Shouldn't we bless them with our presence, with education, health care, and employment opportunities?

If God blesses those who mourn, shouldn't we too? Shouldn't we bless them with listening ears, comforting arms, practical help, and home visits?

If God blesses the humble and pure in heart, shouldn't we? Shouldn't we encourage them in their journeys, and learn from their ways?

If God blesses those who hunger for justice, shouldn't we? Shouldn't we support their fight for a fair wage, or join in their anti-trafficking campaigns?

If God blesses the merciful, shouldn't we? Shouldn't we visit hospitals, rehabilitate prisoners, help the homeless, and befriend the addicted?

If God blesses those who work for peace, shouldn't we? Shouldn't we stand with those who choose non-violent ways to help liberate their oppressed people?

And if God blesses the persecuted, shouldn't we? Shouldn't we support fellow Christians who suffer for their faith, or whistle blowers, or the abused?

As imitators of God (Ephesians 5:1), as students of our Teacher (Luke 6:40), as the arms, ears, and voice of Jesus (1 Corinthians 12:27), we are to be about God's business, blessing what he blesses. As World Vision founder Bob Pierce famously prayed, "Let my heart be broken with the things that break the heart of God."

On that mountainside, as the crowds listen, the children play, and the disciples wonder just what they've gotten themselves into, Jesus extends an invitation to us all: to have our heart expanded as big as God's heart.

Imitate God, therefore, in everything you do,
because you are his dear children.

EPHESIANS 5:1

How often is your heart broken by the things
that break the heart of God?

Who is God stirring you to bless?

COME AND FIND LOVE

And may you have the power to understand, as all God's people should, how wide, how long, how high, and how deep his love is.

EPHESIANS 3:18

God may have a special heart for the vulnerable but we also know that God loves *all* of us. At least we know this in theory. How many of us truly feel it, though? The apostle Paul knew that understanding God's love was a difficult exercise. He believed supernatural revelation was required even to begin (Ephesians 3:16–18). God's love is so large and our comprehension is so small. How can we ever truly understand it?

Part of our problem is that we interpret God's love through human love. If we understand God's love to be anything like the distorted, damaging "love" we've experienced from an abuser, or even the relatively good love of family and friends (at best limited, at worst tainted by mixed motives), we will forever feel cold about God's love for us.

But there is another way. With God's Spirit we may begin to grasp God's love not *by likeness* to human love, but *in contrast* to it. Here's an exercise to try:

Think of the most loving thing someone has done for you. What was it? Perhaps it was a relative forgiving you for something horrible you said, or a colleague opening up a work opportunity for you. Maybe your parents sacrificed greatly so you could go to college, or a friend came to your rescue when you most needed help. Remember the act in detail. Now, even as great as this act of love was, it is tiny in contrast to God's love for you. How tiny?

Picture a grain of sand placed next to a skyscraper.

Compare a single microbe to our largest planet, Jupiter.

Picture the tiniest trickle alongside the mightiest of rivers.

Imagine the faintest scent against the strongest perfume.

The quietest bird call against the loudest thunder clap.

Compare a tiny water drop to the Pacific Ocean.

The flicker of a candle to the blaze of the sun.

A single leaf to a forest of trees . . .

That's how tiny human love is compared to the great love God has for you.

And this love is the breath behind each word of Jesus' Sermon on the Mount, even his toughest ones.

Actually, the truth is far better than what I've written. Paul says God's love can never been fully grasped (Ephesians 3:19), which means any contrast we can suggest between divine and human love will fall short!

God's love for you, then, is literally bigger than you can imagine.

Your unfailing love, O LORD, is as vast as the heavens;
your faithfulness reaches beyond the clouds.

PSALM 36:5

Do you ever struggle to believe God really loves you?
What comparison can you think of to grasp his love for you?

Picture a GRAIN OF SAND placed next to a *skyscraper*.

Compare a SINGLE MICROBE to our

largest planet, *Jupiter*.

Picture the TINIEST TRICKLE alongside

the *mightiest* of rivers.

Imagine the FAINTEST SCENT against

the strongest *perfume*.

The QUIETEST BIRD CALL against the

loudest *thunder clap*.

Compare a TINY WATER DROP

to the Pacific *Ocean*.

The FLICKER OF A CANDLE to the *blaze of the sun*.

A SINGLE LEAF to a *forest* of trees . . .

That's how TINY HUMAN LOVE is compared

to the *great love God has* for you.

COME AND FIND MEANING

"The thief's purpose is to steal and kill and destroy. My purpose is to give them a rich and satisfying life."

JOHN 10:10

Each month, thousands of people type the phrase "meaning of life" into internet search engines.[5] "Why am I here?" they wonder, perhaps in a moment of despair. "What is life all about?" They'll soon find answers ranging from "Life has no meaning" to "The meaning of life is whatever you make it." Thankfully, there is another answer. And it revolves around the meaning of "life" itself.

The New Testament uses two Greek words for "life": *bios*, meaning natural, created life; and *zoë*, meaning God's eternal, supernatural life. We can have *bios* without *zoë*. We can be biologically alive but spiritually dead.[6]

God is an abundant bounty of spiritual life (Genesis 2:7; Exodus 3:14). We were created to have this life inhabit us as a spring fills a well, a fire fills a fireplace, and as God indwelt the temple (see 1 Corinthians 6:19). But with humankind's rebellion from God we severed this source of life. Now a vacant space lies in our hearts—the well has lost its spring, the fireplace has lost its fire, the temple has lost its God, leaving us empty and meaningless.

But then a man came forth from Galilee who offered *zoë* to all (John 1:4). "My purpose is to give them *zoë*," he said of his mission (10:10). To those who believed in him, he promised that "rivers of living water" would flow from their hearts (7:38). He would fill our souls with light (1:9; 8:12), and bring the Father to dwell within us (14:23). Jesus came to unleash the spring in the well, put the fire back into the fireplace, and bring the indwelling God back into the temple of our hearts.

With God's supernatural life now within us, God starts giving us the desire and power to do his work (Philippians 2:13). And He doesn't just give us divine energy to live *by* but a divine mission to live *out*, bringing meaning and purpose to our lives. If we were to put it into a phrase, we could say the real meaning of life is *to live with God*—to have his life within us and have him live his life through us.

In many ways this is what Jesus' Sermon is all about. On that mountain Jesus reveals what *zoë* life looks like in practice—how our callings, relationships, and spirituality are lived out under the direction of God. The Sermon on the Mount is Jesus' manifesto for a meaningful life.

No, the meaning of life is not whatever we make it.

The meaning of life is to live with God and have him live his life through us.

By accepting Jesus' invitation we discover life's deepest purpose.

My old self has been crucified with Christ. It is no longer I who live, but Christ lives in me. So I live in this earthly body by trusting in the Son of God, who loved me and gave himself for me.

GALATIANS 2:20

Have you ever struggled to feel your life has meaning?

If the meaning of life is to live with God, how significant does that make our prayer life?

COME AND FIND SUCCESS

When the seventy-two disciples returned, they joyfully reported to him, "Lord, even the demons obey us when we use your name!" "Yes," he told them, "I saw Satan fall from heaven like lightning!"

LUKE 10:17–18

Before you read any further, attempt to finish the following sentence within ten seconds:

Success is . . .

I have tried this exercise on radio, in churches, and in personal conversations. And in general the answers I've received define success in terms of achievement. So, people have told me success is "being happy," "reaching my goals," "saving souls," or "moving forward and not stagnating." A friend once remarked, "Success is God's prosperity in all areas of my life: spiritual, physical, financial, and relational."

But if we define success as achievement, how do we then measure it? Most of us measure by comparison. Which looks more successful —a church of thirty members or a church of two thousand? A CEO of a multinational company, or a garbage collector? A family with three children, an SUV, and a nice home in the suburbs, or a single mum pushing her newborn in a donated stroller? When defined as achievement and measured by comparison, success seems straightforward: the more happiness felt, goals reached, souls saved, and prosperity achieved, the greater the success in our lives.

After giving his Sermon, Jesus will send his followers out on a mission. When one group of seventy-two excitedly returns from their trip, he takes the opportunity to share a lesson on success. "Lord, even the demons obey us when we use your name!" they say (Luke 10:17). They've seen results, they've tasted success. "I saw Satan fall from heaven like lightning!" Jesus says, affirming their efforts (10:18). The results matter to him. But what Jesus says next no doubt messes with the disciples' definitions of success as much as it messes with ours:

"But don't rejoice because evil spirits obey you; rejoice because your names are registered in heaven" (10:20).

Results are good, but they will come and go.

What matters most is that heaven knows your name.

This upending of success aligns with Jesus' teaching on the mountain where he blesses the most "unsuccessful" of people: the poor, not the self-sufficient; those who mourn, not the happy and affluent; those who hunger for justice, not those who enjoy it; the persecuted, not the victorious. Unsuccessful in the eyes of the world, his blessing declares them successful in the eyes of God. Here is a success based on relationship, not achievement.

Jesus wants us to live fruitful lives (John 15:1–4). Results matter, but they don't matter most. Achievement doesn't define your success and comparison doesn't measure its quantity. For Jesus, success is relational—it's having your name written in heaven's book in God's handwriting (Revelation 3:5). And that is a gift to be received, not an achievement to be made (Ephesians 2:8–9).

Jesus invites us to come and find success.

A success that is more gift than prize.

"Yes, I am the vine; you are the branches. Those who remain in me, and I in them, will produce much fruit. For apart from me you can do nothing."

JOHN 15:5

How often do you compare your success with others?
How can you live out Jesus' definition of success today?

COME AND FIND SECURITY

See how very much our Father loves us, for he calls us his children, and that is what we are! But the people who belong to this world don't recognize that we are God's children because they don't know him.

1 JOHN 3:1

I was on the 436 bus heading into Sydney city when a mid-fifties woman in a faded floral dress hobbled on board at the next stop. She paid her fare, walked up the aisle and, ignoring all the other empty seats, sat down next to me. The bus pulled away and we traveled in silence.

A few moments later Floral Lady did the most extraordinary thing. She turned and looked at me, then thrust her head in my face. And with her brown eyes bulging and her stained teeth bared, she yelled, "I'm alright, aren't I?"

I jumped, and my mind raced for a reply. And because I couldn't think of an appropriate response quickly, I did what any theologically-trained, wholeheartedly devoted follower of Christ would do in such a situation.

I lied.

"Well, *of course* you're alright," I said.

"Some people think I'm funny in the head," she said.

"Now, why would they think *that*?" I asked, knowing full well the answer. She said she didn't know, then fell back into silence.

A few minutes later Floral Lady got up from her seat, crossed the aisle, and sat next to the only other person on the bus. Then she did it again!

"I'm alright, aren't I?"

I wondered how many times that question would be asked throughout the day. And I wondered how deep the anxiety was in that woman's soul—she longed for assurance so desperately she sought it from any old stranger on the bus.

Am I alright? Am I acceptable? Am I lovable? All of us ask such questions. And Jesus' invitation on the mountain addresses them. To all who embrace him Jesus gives the right to become children of God (John 1:12–13). "See how very much our Father loves us," the apostle John says, "for he calls us his children" (1 John 3:1).

You and I are invited to receive a most profound identity. Father God has adopted us, given us his Spirit, and made us heirs to his inheritance (Ephesians 1:5; Galatians 4:6). We may be a success or a failure in the eyes of the world; be rich, poor, happy, or in grief; we may be popular, ridiculed, or socially awkward like Floral Lady; and yet God looks at us and says, "My child." With him we become who we're most deeply meant to be: loved, accepted, and secure.

"I'm alright, aren't I?" we ask anxiously.

"*Of course* you are," Father replies.

And he doesn't lie.

And because we are his children, God has sent the Spirit of his Son into our hearts, prompting us to call out, "Abba, Father." Now you are no longer a slave but God's own child. And since you are his child, God has made you his heir.

GALATIANS 4:6–7

How much do you relate to God as *your* Father, who shares his inheritance with you?

How will you remind yourself today that you are your Father's child?

COME AND MAKE GOD HAPPY

I heard a loud shout from the throne, saying, "Look, God's home is now among his people! He will live with them, and they will be his people. God himself will be with them."

REVELATION 21:3

Saint Augustine famously said that our hearts are restless until they find their rest in God. Human beings long for God, whether they realize it or not. In Revelation 21 we see this longing completely and finally fulfilled—the heart at rest in relationship with its Creator in the coming kingdom of God.

But we spend less time thinking about the longing *God* has—a longing that will also be fulfilled on that great day. Now to be sure, an omnipotent, self-sufficient God doesn't lack anything. We don't meet God's needs. But throughout history God has expressed his own longing in a simple phrase: "You will be my people and I will be your God." We find variations of it throughout scripture:

- "I will claim you as my own people, and I will be your God" (Exodus 6:7).
- "I will be your God, and you will be my people" (Leviticus 26:12).
- "And you will live in Israel, the land I gave your ancestors long ago. You will be my people, and I will be your God" (Ezekiel 36:28).
- "I will put my laws in their minds, and I will write them on their hearts. I will be their God, and they will be my people" (Hebrews 8:10).

For thousands of years God has had one desire—to have a people for himself. This longing has fueled his missionary endeavors: sending prophets to call back his straying people, sending his Son to a windswept mountainside to call the poor, the mourning, the humble, merciful, peacemaking, and persecuted to come into his embrace. In the kingdom of God his desire will finally be fulfilled: "I will be their God, and they will be my children" (Revelation 21:7).

God is our king and judge, for sure. But how often we miss his Father's heart for us—a heart that longs for our free, loving, devoted allegiance. A heart that waits for that longing to be fulfilled.

"But his father said to the servants, 'Quick! Bring the finest robe in the house and put it on him. Get a ring for his finger and sandals for his feet. And kill the calf we have been fattening. We must celebrate with a feast, for this son of mine was dead and has now returned to life. He was lost, but now he is found.'"

LUKE 15:22–24

Is your image of God predominantly one of an "angry" Father or a "longing" Father?

How often do you imagine him being happy?

COME BECAUSE YOU'RE CALLED

"For no one can come to me unless the Father who sent me draws them to me, and at the last day I will raise them up."

JOHN 6:44

At a large church one Sunday, after I'd spoken on how the cross shows God can redeem our broken dreams and suffering, a guy came up to me wanting to talk. "I haven't been to church in twenty-six years," he said. "I've just been through a divorce and a business failure—I have lots of broken dreams. Just this week I said to a friend, 'If there is a God, why doesn't he step in to help?' Then all week I had this feeling I should get to a church service. What you said tonight has really rocked me. It's like I was meant to be here."

A few minutes later a couple walked up. "I haven't been to church in years," the guy said. "And I've *never* been to church," said the girl. "But all this week," the guy said, "we had this strange feeling that we should get to a church service. What you shared tonight was exactly what we needed to hear. It's like we were meant to be here."

These delightful experiences, just moments apart, reminded me that God is always working, drawing people to himself. The Father's desire is that everyone should find salvation in him, so he draws us to Jesus (1 Timothy 2:4; John 6:44). These three people weren't at church by their own decision—they had been wooed there. If they continue to listen to the Father, they will find the eternal life they long for.

God is an inviting God. He draws us to himself. When Jesus sits on the mountain delivering his Sermon, he is only doing what God has always done—inviting us passionately and repeatedly to enter his family. And when we respond to his invitation, it is only because he has first wooed and won us.

"God has drawn you here because he loves you," I told the first guy, before arranging a Bible for him to take home. "When you leave here, you'll find all sorts of distractions placed in your way to ignore what happened tonight. Don't be distracted. God is calling you. Listen to him and find out who Jesus is."

"And when I am lifted up from the earth,
I will draw everyone to myself."

JOHN 12:32

How can you sense God inviting you to follow him each day?
Who is God currently drawing among your family and friends?

A HEART FOR GOD

"God blesses those who are merciful,
for they will be shown mercy.
God blesses those whose hearts are pure,
for they will see God."

MATTHEW 5:7–8

We return to where we began—to the list of people Jesus blesses, the Beatitudes. And there we find the poor in wallet and poor in spirit, the mourning, the merciful, the humble and pure; those who cry out for justice, those who seek to bring peace, and those persecuted for doing right—all are welcomed by Jesus. The invitation is radical. Irrespective of our age, popularity, social status, or earning potential we are invited into God's family. And once we accept, we find forgiveness, restoration, embrace, and reward; love, meaning, success, and security. We are called to be with God, whoever we are. Our places are ready at his table.

We established early on that the Beatitudes are a list of people, not virtues. Jesus isn't asking us to become humble, pure, or merciful here, or poor, mournful, and persecuted. Such people are welcome *despite* these qualities, not because of them. But still, is there anything we can learn from *why* these people are blessed? Is there anything at all we can imitate of them?

Jesus rewrites the rules of blessedness. In his day, someone is considered blessed if he or she lives righteously, has a model family, loves wisdom, keeps the right friends, and is perhaps materially prosperous. But in the Beatitudes Jesus redefines the blessed person as someone who enjoys God's favor, whatever their status, *because of their heart for God.*[7]

Despite their poverty, they worship him.
Despite being persecuted, they obey him.
They are merciful because they follow him.
They are peacemakers because they want to be like him.

According to Jesus, health, wealth, and popularity aren't the true markers of blessedness. He blesses those with a heart for God. And Jesus lives this out personally. He will become impoverished, he will mourn, he will be abused and denied justice, he will be ridiculed for being merciful and living righteously, he will seek peace instead of war and will be persecuted for doing right all because of his heart for the Father. This is what we can imitate: we can have a heart for God.

And it is this kind of heart Jesus says will be resilient.

To build our lives on wealth, status, pride, power, comfort, happiness, or getting our own way is to build our lives on sand (Matthew 7:26–27). Only a heart for God matters. Only a heart for God is resilient. Only this kind of heart has the inner resources to face the toughest storms.

The blessed life is a resilient life.

At its core is a heart for God.

"Oh, that they would always have hearts like this, that they might fear me and obey all my commands! If they did, they and their descendants would prosper forever."

DEUTERONOMY 5:29

What do these rewritten rules of blessedness mean for our ambitions? What area of your life does God want to make more Jesus-shaped?

To build our lives on WEALTH, status, pride,

POWER, comfort, HAPPINESS, or getting our

own way is to build our lives on sand.

Only a *heart for God* matters.

Only a heart for God is RESILIENT. Only this kind of

heart has the inner resources to face the toughest storms.

The BLESSED LIFE is a resilient life.

At its core is a *heart for God*.

PART 2

Your Calling

When God wants to change the world, he doesn't send in the tanks. He sends in the meek, the mourners, those who are hungry and thirsty for God's justice, the peacemakers. . . .

TOM WRIGHT[8]

"You are the salt of the earth. But what good is salt if it has lost its flavor? Can you make it salty again? It will be thrown out and trampled underfoot as worthless.

"You are the light of the world—like a city on a hilltop that cannot be hidden. No one lights a lamp and then puts it under a basket. Instead, a lamp is placed on a stand, where it gives light to everyone in the house. In the same way, let your good deeds shine out for all to see, so that everyone will praise your heavenly Father.

"Don't misunderstand why I have come. I did not come to abolish the law of Moses or the writings of the prophets. No, I came to accomplish their purpose. I tell you the truth, until heaven and earth disappear, not even the smallest detail of God's law will disappear until its purpose is achieved. So if you ignore the least commandment and teach others to do the same, you will be called the least in the Kingdom of Heaven. But anyone who obeys God's laws and teaches them will be called great in the Kingdom of Heaven."

Matthew 5:13–19

CALLED SMALL

"You are the salt of the earth. . . .
You are the light of the world."

MATTHEW 5:13–14

What a motley group are those gathered on that mountainside listening to Jesus. Some have been sick and diseased, others have suffered seizures and chronic pain, some have been paralyzed, and a few have been demon possessed (Matthew 4:24). Jesus looks at them all and says, "You are the salt of the earth" (5:13).

Hundreds have gathered there, rushing from all corners of the region to receive his blessing and get their healing. There are Jews from Jerusalem and Judea, and even Gentiles from Hippos and Gadara.[9] He looks out at them and says, "You are the light of the world" (5:14).

Salt of the earth. Light of the world. Seriously, Jesus, are you sure? What effect could this bunch of peasants have on anything? These insignificant ones? These Gentiles? These little people? He has already blessed them even though they are poor, meek, merciful, humble, sad, disliked, and downtrodden. What kind of influence could such people have in a world that favors power and status? Perhaps he's just being nice to them, saying kind things to lift their self-esteem.

No, he isn't doing that. He'll soon have some tough things to say to them too. Jesus isn't pandering to any sense of psychological victimhood here. He's telling them truth as he sees it—telling them *the* truth. These insignificant ones are the salt that will flavor and preserve society. These humble ones are lights that will draw people to God. These little people are God's chosen agents to bring the world back into harmony with his plans. As history tells it, they will soon turn the world upside down (Acts 17:6 ESV).

In our quiet moments of despair—when we feel like underachievers and nobodies, lacking popularity, platform, political power, or profile, thinking we wield no influence on the world and have little to offer God—let's remember who Jesus proclaimed as the world's reformers: the little people. Common folks. Farmers. Suburbanites. The humble. Not the elite or powerful or the brightest in the class. All these little people had was the blessing of Jesus, a holy distinctiveness, luminescent deeds of love, and the Lord as their center point.

The currency of influence in God's kingdom isn't power in the world but proximity to Jesus. Whatever our quantity of gifts, talents, energy, or influence, he makes us salt and light, doing his work through our hands, giving us a calling in life that is nothing less than grand.

Remember, dear brothers and sisters, that few of you were wise in the world's eyes or powerful or wealthy when God called you. Instead, God chose things the world considers foolish in order to shame those who think they are wise. And he chose things that are powerless to shame those who are powerful.

1 CORINTHIANS 1:26–27

Are you prone to think of yourself as more, or less, than Jesus sees you?

To what degree are you pursuing a holy, distinctive life?

CALLED TO INFLUENCE

"You are the salt of the earth. But what good is salt if it has lost its flavor? Can you make it salty again?"

MATTHEW 5:13

You have a profound calling on your life. As a follower of Jesus you are called to be God's agent of change in the world. This is your ultimate vocation, the career behind any role you perform or job you do. Jesus uses "salt" to describe it. What does he mean by the image? Probably many things, but two popular uses of salt will help us get imaginative about ways to live out this calling.

Think of the salt shaker sitting on your kitchen table. Then think of a butcher curing meat to keep it from going rotten. We use salt every day as a flavor enhancer, and as a preservative to prevent decay. Perhaps Jesus uses this metaphor to describe the dual influence people like you and me are to have on the world in his name.

We are to enhance what is good. Wherever we find goodness, beauty, and truth in our communities—in our homes, offices, universities, and factories, by colleagues, politicians, or those in the media—we should affirm it, amplify it, enhance it. There may be a place for voicing our disapproval at society's ills through a forthright phone call or a letter of protest. But how many of us speak up, write letters, or take to social media with a message of *encouragement* when a public leader does what is right? We are to enhance what is good, wherever we find it.

If we enhance what is good we may find a more welcome audience when we perform our second influential role—to oppose what is bad. We are to halt decay, to stop society from rotting. We are to oppose actions, policies, and products that will bring harm to our neighbor, both next door and across continents. The world may not like us doing this, may even persecute us for doing it—but we are called to serve the world that persecutes us (Matthew 5:10–12; 43–45).

For pastor and statesman John Stott, Jesus' call to be the salt of the earth was nothing less than a call to social justice: to protect the dignity of the individual, provide civil rights for minorities, abolish social and racial discrimination, and care for the poor. "Whenever Christians are conscientious citizens," he said, "they are acting like salt in the community."[10]

Jesus doesn't just call you to be his friend (John 15:15). He calls you to influence society. Enhance what is good. Interrupt what is bad. And for the sake of the world, don't lose your saltiness.

Don't just pretend to love others. Really love them.
Hate what is wrong. Hold tightly to what is good.

ROMANS 12:9

Why do you think Jesus was so firm about
this "salt" not losing its saltiness?

What social causes are you passionate about and committed to?

CALLED TO BE LUMINOUS

"You are the light of the world—
like a city on a hilltop that cannot be hidden."

MATTHEW 5:14

If you didn't grow up in a Christian home, chances are what brought you to faith was not a radio or TV program, a blog post or magazine article, a church sermon or a university debate, but a follower of Jesus who entered your life and shone with a presence beyond this world. Jesus predicts as much. God is described as pure white light (1 John 1:5). Jesus shone with this light (Matthew 17:2). And like a flame passed from candlewick to candlewick, Jesus says his people will radiate this light too. "You are the light of the world—like a city on a hilltop that cannot be hidden" (5:14).

This is the second great calling Jesus gives us. We are to be salt in our communities—enhancing what is good in them, halting what is bad—and we are to be a light to those around us. As salt we influence. As light we illuminate. Just as the lights of a city can be seen for miles, just as we turn on lamps to bring light to a room, so we are called to shine our light publicly. In the workplace, coffee shop, daycare center, or gym, at the shopping mall, book club, university class, or sports ground, we are to shine a light that helps others walk out of darkness.

Our words can bring light to people, revealing truth, offering hope, and sharing the reality of God in creative ways (2 Peter 1:19). But according to Jesus, the things we do can really swing open the door to let out the light within us. "Let your good deeds shine out for all to see," he says, "so that everyone will praise your heavenly Father" (Matthew 5:16). Visiting the sick, serving the poor, helping the unemployed get jobs and the lonely find friends; sponsoring a child, mowing someone's lawn, funding a housing project, or volunteering at a food pantry; offering hospitality, welcoming refugees, rehabilitating prisoners, and going shopping for the elderly—all such acts and more reveal the God who loves our neighbor and now lives within us.

This is what it means to glorify God, by the way. When our lives reflect something of God's own life and light, we glorify—we reveal—him. And he is a most attractive God. That's why people praise him when they see our good works. They recognize another Source behind our words and deeds.

"A Christian has only to *be* in order to change the world," says Christopher Dawson, "for in that act of being, there is contained all the mystery of supernatural life."[11]

So go and be salt, go and be light.

Be a light that sparkles into myriad graceful acts.

"Those who are wise will shine as bright as the sky, and those who lead many to righteousness will shine like the stars forever."

DANIEL 12:3

How have you seen God shine through others?
What practical act will you do this week to reveal the goodness of God?

CALLED TO LOVE

Jesus replied, "'You must love the LORD your God with all your heart, all your soul, and all your mind.' This is the first and greatest commandment. A second is equally important: 'Love your neighbor as yourself.'"

MATTHEW 22:37–39

A friend and I once did an eight-day pilgrimage from Lindisfarne Island to Durham Cathedral in the north of England. Much of our second day's walk was done in view of Dunstanburgh Castle. This fourteenth-century fort may be in ruins, but it remains the largest castle in Northumberland. Built to be seen from every angle, it is an impressive sight seven centuries later.

Dunstanburgh Castle was built by Thomas, Earl of Lancaster, with one purpose: to declare Thomas's wealth and glory to the district. In many ways he succeeded. Hundreds of years after his death, the castle he built keeps his name alive. But in the most important sense he failed. The sign out front of the castle that describes Thomas to visitors remembers him as an "arrogant and unpopular" man.

When we talk about our calling in life it's easy to go straight to the grand things we'd like to achieve—the books we'll write, the businesses we'll start, the churches we'll plant, the "castles" we'll leave behind us. You may well birth something that lives on after you're gone. But it won't be the most important part of your legacy.

We are called to be salt. We are called to be light. And both spring from a more fundamental calling: the call to love. "'You must love the LORD your God with all your heart, all your soul, and all your mind.' . . . 'Love your neighbor as yourself'" (Matthew 22:37–39). Jesus says there is no greater calling for us to live out. Love is the law behind all laws (22:40), and the ground beneath everything he discusses in his Sermon. Love God. Love others. The rest are details.

Love for God comes first for two good reasons. We are to obey him above all others (Acts 5:29) and we are to love him before all others (Exodus 20:3; Matthew 10:37) because he is God, infinitely good, and no one else is worthy of the honor. But secondly, by loving God first we love others better. God's essence is love; by worshipping him we become more loving (1 John 4:7–12). Love for God and love for others are intricately linked.

So imagine that after you die a sign is placed outside your house telling visitors about you. What does the sign say? Beyond the "castles" you built and things you achieved, how does it describe you? As someone who achieved much but loved little, or as someone who achieved much by loving much?

In the end, the castles we build for ourselves will crumble.

All that will remain of our lives is love.

Love God. Love others.

The rest are details.

Three things will last forever—faith, hope, and love—and the greatest of these is love.

1 CORINTHIANS 13:13

How can this calling to love be fulfilled through your daily work?

What if you reviewed each day by how much you loved rather than what you accomplished?

CALLED AND EMPOWERED

Don't be drunk with wine, because that will ruin your life. Instead, be filled with the Holy Spirit.

EPHESIANS 5:18

Here's what our lives are to be about: we're here to be salt that enhances the God-flavors of the earth, light that reveals the God-colors of the world, and love that brings the unseen God into view.[12] We are to fill the world with good things, whether through words or acts, talking or listening, making or helping, work or play.

But to fill the world with good things we must first be filled with good things. We can't dispense what we don't have. To be salt, light, and love we must be filled with the God who has these qualities and more. And this requires only one thing from us.

Notice for a moment how much the Holy Spirit responds to empty spaces. We see the Spirit first in the book of Genesis, hovering over the formless, empty world (Genesis 1:2). He is then breathed into empty human beings (2:7). He fills the empty temple with his presence (2 Chronicles 5:11–14). He fills Jesus, who emptied himself of privilege (Matthew 3:13–16; Philippians 2:7). He fills the disciples at Pentecost, empty of courage (John 20:19; Acts 2:1–4). We're told to bring our thirsty souls for the Spirit to quench and to offer our empty bodies as his temple (John 7:37–39; 1 Corinthians 6:19). We're not to fill our hearts with wine but fill them with the Spirit (Ephesians 5:18). The Spirit loves to fill a vacuum.

If this is true, then it follows there is such a thing as holy emptiness—an emptiness reserved for him. We can be filled with the Holy Spirit by offering him this emptiness and making sure nothing else takes his place.

Many things vie with the Spirit for our emptiness. Wine is only one of them. Pride, greed, bitterness, and lust seek to fill that space, as do the worries, dreams, and plans that so often consume us. TV, magazines, and social media chatter can fill us with noise. And most of us are experts at filling our lives with ourselves.

Is there space in your heart for the Holy Spirit? Will you make space for him? The good news is we can. Confession clears out sin and makes space for the Spirit (1 John 1:9). Forgiveness removes the blockage of bitterness (Colossians 3:13). Worship empties our hearts of ourselves (Psalm 63:1–4), and prayer makes space for his voice (1 Samuel 3:1–10). When he comes he fills us with power, boldness, and supernatural abilities (Acts 2:42–47) and love, joy, goodness, and self-control (Galatians 5:22–23).

The Holy Spirit loves to bring his dynamic, creative presence to empty spaces. Let's give him what he wants: our emptiness to fill, empowering us to be his salt, light, and love to the world.

> After this prayer, the meeting place shook, and they were all filled with the Holy Spirit. Then they preached the word of God with boldness.
>
> ACTS 4:31

What is taking up the Spirit's space in your heart?
Will you hand that space back to God now?

CALLED AND GIFTED

A spiritual gift is given to each of us so we can help each other.

1 CORINTHIANS 12:1–11

Some years ago I interviewed music legend Andraé Crouch. With his band The Disciples, Andraé was one of the pioneers of the gospel music genre and worked on albums for Michael Jackson, Diana Ross, Madonna, and Stevie Wonder. But there was a twist to his success:

Andraé couldn't read a note of music.

The story goes like this. When Andraé was a child, his businessman father, Benjamin Sr., tested a calling to preach by taking a Sunday service at a small church. With ten people in the service and no piano player, Benjamin Sr. surprised Andraé by calling him out in front of the congregation. Andraé was eleven years old, had a bad stutter, and suffered from dyslexia. He was shy and withdrawn. Andraé had no idea what his father was about to do.

"Andraé," he said, "if God was to give you the gift of music, would you use it for his glory for the rest of your life?"

"Ye-e-a-a-h-h, daddy," Andraé stuttered out.

His father laid his hands on Andraé and prayed. If Andraé received the gift of music Benjamin Sr. would also take it as a sign he was to give up his business and pastor full time.

When the congregation requested Benjamin's preaching again, the family returned to the little church for a further three Sundays. On the final week Benjamin Sr. again called his son out to the front.

"Well," he said, "if you're going to play, *play!*"

Andraé couldn't believe his ears. While he loved music, the closest he'd come to touching a piano was a cardboard toy his mother had bought him. Benjamin Sr. swiveled the piano stool to Andraé's height, explained what the pedals did, and sat him in front of the keys. The congregation then began singing the old hymn "What a Friend We Have in Jesus," Andraé cautiously reached for the keyboard . . . and began to play along with both hands.[13]

Andraé's experience is exceptional, I know. But according to scripture, *all* of us are given special abilities by the Holy Spirit to accomplish his work (1 Corinthians 12:7). Some of these spiritual gifts are dramatic, like speaking in unknown languages and working miracles (12:10)—or playing an instrument you've never learned before. Others are less so, like gifts of serving, teaching, giving, or encouraging (Romans 12:7–8). Whether "spectacular" or "ordinary," each gift is from God and not to be neglected.

We are not called to be salt, light, and love in the world by our own strength or talent alone. The Holy Spirit empowers us to do the extraordinary. If you don't know what gifts you have, start by becoming acquainted with the variety of gifts mentioned in the Bible,[14] then experiment with some by serving others and getting feedback. Joy and effectiveness will be clues as to which gifts are yours.

You may not be able to sit at a piano and play fluently without lessons. But God wants to do his work through you in ways that only he can.

You are not just called. You are gifted.

Do you have the gift of speaking? Then speak as though God himself were speaking through you. Do you have the gift of helping others? Do it with all the strength and energy that God supplies. Then everything you do will bring glory to God through Jesus Christ.

1 PETER 4:11

Do you know what gifts God has given you?

How are you using them?

CALLED TO COMMUNITY

All of you together are Christ's body, and each of you is a part of it.

1 CORINTHIANS 12:27

I love the story of the seventh-century poet Caedmon. Originally a farmhand at Whitby Abbey in the north of England, Caedmon had an extraordinary dream one night. In the dream a man asked him to sing a song about creation. Being a farmer and not a musician, Caedmon shyly refused. But the man in the dream assured Caedmon he could do it, and as the dream progressed Caedmon did compose a song praising the Creator of all:

Now [we] must honor the guardian of heaven,
the might of the architect, and his purpose,
the work of the father of glory
as he, the eternal lord, established the beginning of wonders . . .

Upon waking the next morning, Caedmon found he was able to recall this song in detail. He told his foreman about the experience, who then took him to see the abbess, Hilda. Hilda listened carefully to Caedmon's story, then gave him a task: produce another poem, this time based on a verse of scripture. Caedmon returned the next day with the new poem.

Recognizing Caedmon's divine gift, Hilda ordered her scholars to teach him history and the Bible. Each day he was tasked with writing a new poem. We're told by the ancient historian Bede that after a night's reflection on the scripture given to him, Caedmon would create verses with such "sweetness and humility" they moved people to worship and conversion.[15]

Caedmon's story beautifully illustrates the connection between calling and community. Caedmon, a simple monastery farmhand, was nevertheless a part of Christ's "body," the church (1 Corinthians 12:12–31). The Holy Spirit gave him a gift and that gift was confirmed by the believers around him—first by his foreman, then by

Hilda. Having recognized the gift, Hilda helped fan it into flame by giving Caedmon training and opportunities to serve (2 Timothy 1:6). Whitby Abbey then became Caedmon's base for sharing his gift with the world.

We are called, we are empowered, we are gifted. And all of this happens within the church, Christ's body. Like Caedmon, our calling is discovered and our gifting is confirmed in the context of Christian community.

A simple farm hand given an extraordinary ability—Caedmon was one of the "little people" Jesus loves to use. But he didn't serve alone. He was part of Christ's body.

And we too are called to community.

He makes the whole body fit together perfectly. As each part does its own special work, it helps the other parts grow, so that the whole body is healthy and growing and full of love.

EPHESIANS 4:16

Are you committed to a local church or faith community?
How have others confirmed gifting in you, and you in them?

CALLED TO DREAM

Then I saw a new heaven and a new earth, for the old heaven and the old earth had disappeared.

REVELATION 21:1

If you and I were to talk awhile and I were to pry into your soul, it wouldn't take long for me to discover you have dreams. You want to become someone. You want to achieve something. You have goals and aspirations you want to fulfill. And if I were to pry a little further, we might trace each dream back to its inspiration—to the book, hero, experience, or film that first gave you a glimpse of what to aim for. Dreams are like that: they call us toward the future based on something we've already seen.

God has a dream for the world. This dream is no mere wish; its fulfillment is promised. His dream is a new heaven and earth, and he is guiding all history toward it. We don't know exactly what this dream will look like, but God has given us a glimpse. And this dream of God's can inspire our dreams too.

God's dream is a place of fulfilled longings. Advertisers may shout loudly, but our deepest desires will never be satisfied with another trip to the shopping mall. As Blaise Pascal intimated, there's a God-shaped hole in the heart that only God can fill. "Look, God's home is now among his people! He will live with them, and they will be his people" (Revelation 21:3). In God's dream, *our* longing is fulfilled.

God's dream is a place of healed wounds. Every tear will be wiped from our eyes as there will be no more mourning or pain (21:4). Death, disability, and illness will be gone (Isaiah 35:5–6; 65:20), and our groaning earth will be made well (Romans 8:18–23). Streams will flow in the desert, flowers will blossom, droughts and floods will cease (Isaiah 35:1, 6). Earth and humanity will be made whole in God's fulfilled dream.

God's dream is a place of radiant beauty. The new heavens and earth will gleam with God's own beauty—a glory like the most dazzling of jewels (Revelation 4:3; 21:11, 18). The new creation isn't only about goodness. Its aesthetics will be overwhelming.

And God's dream is a place of restored harmony. There will be harmony between nations as they walk in God's light and turn their swords into gardening tools (Revelation 21:24; Isaiah 2:4). There will be economic justice for the poor (Isaiah 11:4; 65:21–23), and harmony between animals (11:6). God's dream is a place of peace.

In his Sermon on the Mount, Jesus will soon call us to pray for God's dream to become a reality—on earth as in heaven; now, not just then. What if God's dream inspired us to become pastors and missionaries to help fulfill spiritual longing? Or nurses and therapists to help heal people's wounds? Or designers and filmmakers to help spread God's beauty? Or aid workers and politicians to help restore God's harmony? The possibilities are many, the career opportunities endless. Whether as a full-time worker or a volunteer, if we do good work in Jesus' name we can be part of God's dream coming true.

"May your Kingdom come soon.
May your will be done on earth,
as it is in heaven."

MATTHEW 6:10

What dreams do you have for your life?
To what degree are they shaped by God's dream for the future?

CALLED TO LISTEN

And the LORD came and called as before, "Samuel! Samuel!"
And Samuel replied, "Speak, your servant is listening."

1 SAMUEL 3:10

What do we know about the crowd that gathered to hear Jesus speak on the mountain? We know they were "little" people, small in the eyes of the world. We know that despite their status, they had a heart for God. And we know they were keen to hear Jesus. While healing may have been their first motivation for coming (Matthew 4:24), they stayed for Jesus' Sermon and were soon astounded at his words (7:28–29).

To hear the call of God we must want to listen. But without Jesus' physical presence with us, how do we do that? An Old Testament story may be helpful.

Young Samuel is sleeping in the tabernacle (1 Samuel 3:3). As biblical scholars tell us, the location is significant. In the ancient world one hoped to discover God's plans by sleeping where God was thought to dwell. Samuel wants to hear from God.

Samuel is woken by a voice calling his name: "Samuel!" Notice that he recognizes the words being spoken. The voice isn't speaking Italian, Swahili, or the language of angels, but Samuel's own tongue. It is a "human" voice he hears. Samuel even mistakes it as the voice of Eli the priest.

Samuel hears the voice call again: "Samuel!" Again he runs to Eli, and again Eli tells him he's mistaken and should return to sleep.

Samuel had been dedicated to God as a baby and already serves in the temple (1:11–28; 2:18), but he doesn't yet know the Lord (3:7). He doesn't recognize this voice as being God's voice. Only when the mysterious experience happens a third time does Eli realize it is God who is speaking. He then guides Samuel in how to respond: "If someone calls again, say, 'Speak, LORD, your servant is listening'" (3:9).

This story tells us much about hearing God's voice today:

1. God speaks to those who are in a position to hear him.
2. God speaks in ways we'll understand.
3. We need mature believers to help us differentiate God's voice from others.

Along the course of our lives there will be much need for God's guidance. Should we marry? If so, who? What career path should we choose? God may use a verse of scripture to guide us, or the words of a friend, an uncanny coincidence, or a gentle whisper. Though sometimes cryptic and often costly to obey, his guidance will be intelligible to us and godly mentors will help us understand it.

But our first task in hearing God's voice is to develop a listening posture, just like Samuel in the tabernacle, Moses in the Tent (Exodus 33:7–9), Elijah on the mountaintop (1 Kings 19:11–12), and Mary sitting at her Lord's feet (Luke 10:38–42).

With Samuel we say, "Speak, Lord, your servant is listening."

With the crowd on the mountainside, we listen.

Before daybreak the next morning, Jesus got up
and went out to an isolated place to pray.

MARK 1:35

Do you have a special place where you meet
God to read scripture and pray?

How often do you make time to hear from God?

CALLED TO LEAD

"Reign over the fish in the sea, the birds in the sky, and all the animals that scurry along the ground."

GENESIS 1:28

During a holiday, my young nieces introduced me to a favorite TV show of theirs, *The Dog Whisperer*. In the series, an intuitive animal behaviorist named Cesar Millan gives advice to people with unruly dogs. I soon became hooked on the show.

But I didn't need to watch many episodes to recognize that whatever the problem—a dog endlessly chasing its tail, or barking all day, or getting aggressive toward visitors, or attacking other dogs in the street—Cesar's advice was largely the same: each owner had to exercise calm but assertive leadership over the dog. When owners treated their dogs as equals (which many did) or as surrogate children (which many *more* did), the dogs filled the leadership void and started ruling the home. But when given training, discipline, and (only then) affection, peace was restored and the dogs themselves became happier.

I realized something while watching *The Dog Whisperer*. Consciously or not, what Cesar Millan was really doing was teaching what is often called the "creation mandate." When God told Adam and Eve to "Reign over the fish in the sea, the birds in the sky, and all the animals that scurry along the ground" (Genesis 1:28), he was putting humanity in charge of the animal world. And when God placed them in Eden to "tend and watch over it" (2:15), he was calling humanity to cultivate the earth. Ruling the animals, cultivating the earth—in submission to God, we are to exercise God-like leadership over his creation. This is what being made in God's "image" means (1:27).

But humanity slipped out of submission to God, distorted its divine image, and upset all other relationships as a result. Instead of cultivating the earth we have often destroyed it through greed. Instead of ruling the animals we have often abused them or made them equals. Humans must lead well for creation to flourish.

Jesus came to restore our humanity and renew God's image within us (Colossians 3:9–10). By submitting to him we once again imitate his caring rule: nurturing the animal world by leading it well, cultivating the earth to be fruitful and sustainable. And the principle applies to occupations beyond zoology and forestry. Anything we create, organize, or govern—whether a home, a business, a football team, or a city council—is to be led as if God himself were leading it.

Cesar Millan doesn't really train dogs. He trains humans—to take their assigned role in God's world seriously. And as Jesus in his hillside Sermon teaches us to be salt, light, and love, he is calling us to take our leadership role seriously.

To lead in our occupations as he would lead in them.

To exercise godly authority.

To lead, nurture, and cultivate.

For we are God's masterpiece. He has created us anew in Christ Jesus, so we can do the good things he planned for us long ago.

EPHESIANS 2:10

How are you leading and caring for God's creation?
How can you exercise godly leadership today, whatever your role?

CALLED TO GUIDE

You are royal priests, a holy nation, God's very own possession. As a result, you can show others the goodness of God, for he called you out of the darkness into his wonderful light.

1 PETER 2:9

She's been a TV phenomenon, launched magazines and cable channels, packed out stadiums with her events, and enrolled millions in her self-help courses. She may be one of the most successful businesswomen in history, but Oprah Winfrey's self-description is rather more religious. "I am the messenger to deliver the message of redemption," she said in an interview—"of hope, of forgiveness, of gratitude, of evolving people to the best of themselves."[16] To her devoted audience Oprah's advice is tantamount to holy revelation. To many, she has become the high priestess of religion-less spirituality.[17]

When a secular world rejects the church, it doesn't forgo spiritual direction. It just seeks it elsewhere. While it may ignore priests dressed in robes (or pastors dressed in suits), it will soon start looking for "priests" of another kind for help navigating life. It might be a favorite author, a fortune-teller, or a talk show host like Oprah who offers "hope" and "redemption." Psychotherapists have become modern priests, listening to our anxieties and offering healing. Motivational speakers tour the country offering "sermons" in the form of life tips and inspiration.

We all need guidance. We all need a priest.

Spiritual beings have always needed spiritual leaders.

When God founded the nation of Israel he established a priesthood that would mediate his voice and forgiveness to the people (Numbers 3:5–9). When Jesus came to earth he came as the ultimate priest, mediating God's voice and forgiveness to us (Hebrews 2:17). And when Jesus recruits us into his mission, he sends *us* out as priests, to speak God's words and extend his forgiveness too (1 Peter 2:5).

Just think about that for a moment. People are searching for spiritual guides and you and I are sent forth as priests. We don't need robes or collars, just holiness and humility (1 Peter 2:11; 5:5). We don't need degrees and ordination, just gentleness and preparation (3:15–16). We are the salt of the earth, we are the light of the world . . .

And we are to be priests to our neighbors.

A friend of mine has discovered a new calling—to be a "chaplain" to his street. Mike spends time with his neighbors, babysits their kids, offers practical help to those who need it, and visits the sick. He listens to people's hopes and fears, and prays for anyone who'll accept it. It's not surprising that conversations about God are starting to develop. Mike is being a priest.

You are God's priestly guide, called to "show others the goodness of God" (2:9). Who are you being God's voice to? Who are you extending his forgiveness to? Who are you helping to guide into the light?

Many a life has been changed over a coffee table chat with a Spirit-filled friend.

"And you have caused them to become
a Kingdom of priests for our God.
And they will reign on the earth."

REVELATION 5:10

Who are you being God's voice to?
Who could you become a "chaplain" to this week?

CALLED TO LIVE RIGHTLY

"Don't misunderstand why I have come. I did not come to abolish the law of Moses or the writings of the prophets. No, I came to accomplish their purpose."

MATTHEW 5:17

In my early twenties I had a revelation. Driving to work one day, I realized that road rules were there for our benefit. A speed limit had been set not to hamper my freedom or prove I was a lawbreaker, but to protect me and those around me. If I sped and lost control of my car, I could hurt myself, the person driving toward me, or someone on the sidewalk. Those laws were in place because human life is valuable and should be protected.

I made a similar discovery over the Ten Commandments. This "law of Moses" was meant to protect life and help people flourish. You cannot flourish when your life is in danger (Exodus 20:13), when your belongings have been stolen (20:15), or when you're being pursued by a stalker (20:17). You cannot flourish by working without a break (20:8–11) or worshipping anything else but God (20:1–6).

So it's no surprise that Jesus says he hasn't come to abolish the law of Moses (Matthew 5:17). It serves an important purpose. Vices like theft, murder, and idolatry were just as destructive after Jesus came as they were before, so why take away the guard rails? What Jesus comes to do is *accomplish* this law, to fulfill it. To fill it up with meaning, restore its life-protecting intent, and wrestle it back from some of the religious teachers of his day who have turned it into a system of merit-keeping with God. As we'll see, this is what Jesus does in the rest of his Sermon.

But while Jesus says the law isn't to be abolished, neither is it to be our focus. We're not to ferret out every injunction in the Old Testament so we can follow it scrupulously. Our focus is Jesus, not the law. Jesus is the law's fulfillment, and he collapses all of Moses' laws into just two commands: to love God and to love others. By following Jesus and living a life of love, the law is taken care of.

In the case of speeding, the law of the land aligns with the law of God. But many times it won't—our country's laws will often permit what God does not. In his Sermon, Jesus calls us to live rightly for our own sake and for others'. But for us, he defines what "right" is.

> Love does no wrong to others, so love fulfills
> the requirements of God's law.
>
> ROMANS 13:10

Who defines what is right and wrong for you in practice?
How is the Spirit calling you to change today?

CALLED TO LIVE BRAVELY

The Lord had said to Abram, "Leave your native country, your relatives, and your father's family, and go to the land that I will show you."

GENESIS 12:1

The African impala is a deer-like animal that can jump to a height of around ten feet (over three meters) and cover a distance of around thirty-six feet (more than eleven meters). Yet the impala can be kept in any zoo enclosure with just a three-foot-high wall. Why? Because it isn't tall enough to peer over the barrier, and if it can't see where its feet will land, it won't jump.

That's like a lot of us. We won't take a leap of faith unless we can see where we'll land, so we rarely taste the adventure the Christian life is meant to be. But if we're to follow the One who calls us to be salt, light, and love to the world, the One who calls us to dream, listen, lead, and guide, we'll soon be called to leap from our comfortable lives into risky, unknown places.

Our guide in this is Abraham, who leaps bravely when the call of God comes (Genesis 12:1–8). He is seventy-five at the time. He is childless (11:30). He is called to leave home at an age when security is precious and is promised a child when the idea seems ludicrous. And yet God gives no details as to the "where" or "how" of this calling's fulfillment, saying only, "Go to the land that I will show you. I will make you into a great nation" (12:1–2).

Leap from the enclosure, Abraham—leap!

I will guide your feet, but first you must leap.

Imagine being Abraham, trying to explain God's call to those around you. Imagine the quizzical look in their eyes, the smirks on their faces, the whispers behind your back, and even your own questions. Like those called to build boats on dry land (Genesis 6:9–22), or heal crippled beggars (Acts 3:1–8), or pray for well-known murderers (Acts 9:10–18), or feed thousands with a few scraps (Mark 6:30–44), such leaps of faith rarely make sense to others.

But Abraham leaps nonetheless. He sets out in faith, soon finds his land, later has his son, and ultimately sires a nation. God guides Abraham's feet, but only once he's leaped.

On three occasions now God has called me to leap from my own comfortable enclosure. In each case I've left a secure job without knowing what lay ahead.

Leap from the enclosure, Sheridan—leap!

I will guide your feet, but first you must leap.

And in each case God has led me to a place of greater service and impact.

I'm not your role model, though. In each case I've fretted about money and worried what the future held. Each time I've been more impala than Abraham.

But I have learned this much about walking by faith: that we'll rarely know the outcome before we make the leap, that we'll rarely know the destination before we begin to walk, that we'll rarely see the miracle before building the boat, offering to pray, or beginning to share our loaves and fishes.

We are called to be salt, light, and love to the world. We are called to dream, listen, lead, and guide. And all this requires that we leap bravely when he calls.

Faith is the confidence that what we hope for will actually happen; it gives us assurance about things we cannot see.

HEBREWS 11:1

When did God last call you to take a leap of faith?
What barrier are you hiding behind?

If we're to follow the *One* who calls us to be SALT, LIGHT, and LOVE to the world, the *One* who calls us to DREAM, LISTEN, LEAD, and GUIDE, we'll soon be called to leap from our comfortable lives into risky, unknown places.

CALLED TO BRING WHAT WE HAVE

"How much bread do you have?" he asked.
"Go and find out." They came back and reported,
"We have five loaves of bread and two fish."

MARK 6:38

A farmer's crop is a provision from God (Deuteronomy 16:15), yet the farmer is required to harvest it. Each child born is a gift from God (Genesis 33:5), yet no pregnancy takes place without the union of husband and wife. Israel's wars were won by God (Joshua 10:42), but Israel needed to fight them. In work, procreation, and the battles of life, God works with us in a divine-human partnership. And the same is true of our callings. We don't work alone, and neither does God. We bring what we have and he blesses it.

This principle is vividly portrayed in the story of the loaves and fishes. When Jesus later finds an enormous crowd at Bethsaida, a practical matter arises about catering. The tired disciples, originally brought here for some rest, panic when Jesus tells them to feed the masses themselves. They have only a few loaves of bread and a couple of fish among them. But Jesus takes what they have and miraculously feeds the stadium-size crowd.

Now, notice a few things about the story:

- Who is to feed the crowd? The disciples. Jesus doesn't say *"I'll* feed them," but *"You* feed them" (Mark 6:37).
- Whose food is to be used? The disciples'. Jesus doesn't make fish and bread fall from the sky but takes and uses what they have.
- And who is to arrange the people, distribute the food and clean up afterwards? The disciples (6:39, 41, 43).
- But who does the miracle? Jesus does. He directs the whole event. He is the one who blesses the bread and fish and provides an endless supply for the disciples to distribute (6:41).

Jesus could harvest a field, create a child, or win a battle without any human involvement. But in general he does his work—even his miraculous work—through the actions of little people like you and me. A crowd is fed when the disciples pass out bread. A church is born as Peter stands to speak (Acts 2:36–41). Ananias prays and Paul receives his sight (9:17–18). Philip answers questions and a eunuch discovers Christ (8:26–39).

We don't work alone but in a divine-human partnership. And Jesus' way of working is to take the little we have and bless it. So bring him your proverbial loaves and fishes—bring him what measure of gifts, talents, and skills you have, what endowment of time, health, and energy you've been given, what finances, possessions, and wisdom you've acquired—and watch him miraculously multiply them.

So David triumphed over the Philistine with only a sling and a stone, for he had no sword.

1 SAMUEL 17:50

Have you ever thought your gifts, talents, and resources too small for God to use?

Have you offered all you have back to him?

A HIGH CALLING

"But what good is salt if it has lost its flavor?
Can you make it salty again? . . .
No one lights a lamp and then puts it under a basket. . . .
So if you ignore the least commandment and teach others to do the same, you will be called the least in the Kingdom of Heaven."

MATTHEW 5:13, 15, 19

All of history can be gathered up into one grand story. This story begins with a God who creates a world teeming with creatures, flowers, color, and light, with his image-bearing humans as his coworkers (Genesis 1–2). It continues with a great rebellion unleashing evil and disorder into the world (Genesis 3), to which God launches a recovery mission, calling the nation Israel to be his guiding light (12:1–3; Isaiah 9:1–2). The story reaches its peak with God visiting earth himself, accepting our ridicule and his own crucifixion, then rising from death to offer forgiveness and new life (2 Corinthians 5:17–19). It will ultimately end with this restoration complete—in a new world of fulfilled longings, healed wounds, radiant beauty, and restored harmony (Revelation 21–22).

To follow Jesus means being swept into this grand drama of God reconciling the world to himself. He has written us into the script; he has called us into the cast. And he hasn't just called us but empowered us, gifted us, positioned us, urging us to leap bravely into each scene and sit at pianos we never knew we could play. Enhancing the good, halting the bad, loving God above all and loving others as God would—as we act as salt, light, and love to this world, as subplots unfold of prodigal sons coming home, Jesus ushers this grand story to its ending.

The calling is serious, the requirements are high. They may be poor, meek, justice-seeking "little people" on that mountainside, but Jesus doesn't insult their intelligence, diminish their dignity, or belittle them as victims by lowering his demands. He speaks to them, and to us, with bone-shaking clarity. Salt without taste will be thrown away (Matthew 5:13), a light that doesn't shine is useless (5:15). Ignore Jesus and his commands and we will be least in his kingdom (5:19). This story is too important for characters who won't play their part.

Such words cut across any self-centered sentiments we may have about finding our life's calling. This is God's story, not ours. We follow Jesus' agenda, not our own. He wants total surrender, absolute commitment. We benefit, no doubt, but only when he's first.

A variety of voices competes for our attention each day—from advertisers, columnists, celebrities, and activists, from priests, politicians, and cable TV hosts, from family, friends, colleagues, and spouses, and from all those desires and worries that whisper deep inside us. "Pursue me!" "Buy me!" "This is the way to life," they say. But the One who listened intently and spoke only what he heard (John 14:10, 24), did only as he was told (5:19), whatever the cost (Luke 22:42), calls us to hear one voice above all others—his own.

The resilient life is one attuned to the voice of Jesus.

Who calls us to play our part in his unfolding story.

"My sheep listen to my voice; I know them, and they follow me."

JOHN 10:27

Whose "voice" most influences your decisions?

Is Jesus' agenda yours?

PART 3

Your Relationships

Can we become light, salt, and leaven to our brothers and sisters in the human family? Can we offer hope, courage, and confidence to the people of this era? Do we dare break through our paralyzing fear? Will people be able to say of us, "See how they love each other, how they serve their neighbor, and how they pray to their Lord?"

HENRI NOUWEN[18]

"But I warn you—unless your righteousness is better than the righteousness of the teachers of religious law and the Pharisees, you will never enter the Kingdom of Heaven!

"You have heard that our ancestors were told, 'You must not murder. If you commit murder, you are subject to judgment.' But I say, if you are even angry with someone, you are subject to judgment! If you call someone an idiot, you are in danger of being brought before the court. And if you curse someone, you are in danger of the fires of hell.

"So if you are presenting a sacrifice at the altar in the Temple and you suddenly remember that someone has something against you, leave your sacrifice there at the altar. Go and be reconciled to that person. Then come and offer your sacrifice to God.

"When you are on the way to court with your adversary, settle your differences quickly. Otherwise, your accuser may hand you over to the judge, who will hand you over to an officer, and you will be thrown into prison. And if that happens, you surely won't be free again until you have paid the last penny.

"You have heard the commandment that says, 'You must not commit adultery.' But I say, anyone who even looks at a woman with lust has already committed adultery with her in his heart. So if your eye—even your good eye—causes you to lust, gouge it out and throw it away. It is better for you to lose one part of your body than for your whole body to be thrown into hell. And if your hand—even your stronger hand—causes you to sin, cut it off and throw it away. It is better for you to lose one part of your body than for your whole body to be thrown into hell.

"'You have heard the law that says, 'A man can divorce his wife by merely giving her a written notice of divorce.' But I say that a man who divorces his wife, unless she has been unfaithful, causes her to commit adultery. And anyone who marries a divorced woman also commits adultery.

"You have also heard that our ancestors were told, 'You must not break your vows; you must carry out the vows you make to the LORD.' But I say, do not make any vows! Do not say, 'By heaven!' because heaven is God's throne. And do not say, 'By the earth!' because the earth is his footstool. And do not say, 'By Jerusalem!' for Jerusalem is the city of the great King. Do not even say, 'By my head!' for you can't turn one hair white or black. Just say a simple, 'Yes, I will,' or 'No, I won't.' Anything beyond this is from the evil one.

"You have heard the law that says the punishment must match the injury: 'An eye for an eye, and a tooth for a tooth.' But I say, do not resist an evil person! If someone slaps you on the right cheek, offer the other cheek also. If you are sued in court and your shirt is taken from you, give your coat, too. If a soldier demands that you carry his gear for a mile, carry it two miles. Give to those who ask, and don't turn away from those who want to borrow.

"You have heard the law that says, 'Love your neighbor' and hate your enemy. But I say, love your enemies! Pray for those who persecute you! In that way, you will be acting as true children of your Father in heaven. For he gives his sunlight to both the evil and the good, and he sends rain on the just and the unjust alike. If you love only those who love you, what reward is there for that? Even corrupt tax collectors do that much. If you are kind only to your friends, how are you different from anyone else? Even pagans do that. But you are to be perfect, even as your Father in heaven is perfect."

Matthew 5:20–48

HOLY HEARTS

"But I warn you—unless your righteousness is better than the righteousness of the teachers of religious law and the Pharisees, you will never enter the Kingdom of Heaven!"

MATTHEW 5:20

Deep within you is a holy place—the place of your deepest desires and your truest self; a space where God comes to reside and speak. This place is deeper down than your emotions, although it affects what you feel; deeper than your thoughts, although it shapes your ideas and speech. It is the place where beliefs reside and actions spring. It is the center of your very existence.

Some people call it the soul. Others call it the self. Jesus calls it the heart, and as he sits on that mountain looking down the grassy plains to the Sea of Galilee, looking over the people gathered before him—fathers, mothers, sisters, brothers, colleagues, and friends in a web of relationships—he reminds them with the strongest words of the heart's importance.

The religious leaders of Jesus' day, the Pharisees, are experts at good deeds. They've calculated 613 commandments within the Jewish law and aspire to obey them all. But for many of them, their expertise is in outward conformity rather than purity of heart. They don't murder, but they do hate (Matthew 5:21–22; 43–44). They don't commit adultery, but they do lust (5:27–28). They give to the poor, but do so to look good (6:1–2). They do the right things from wrong hearts—and Jesus calls his people to a higher standard than this (5:20). Deeds matter but motives matter more.

We are to love God with all our heart. God's words should sink deeply into our heart (Luke 8:15). Our treasures reveal the state of our heart (Matthew 6:21). A good person produces good things from their heart (12:35). The words on our lips reflect what's in our heart (15:18–19).

Heart, heart, heart.

Jesus is all about the heart.

And this will be apparent in all he says next about anger, lust, and hate and their destructive potential in our friendships, marriages, and communities. We are to be people of integrity, he says, having congruence between our motives and actions.

This calls for careful reflection from you and me, as we too can be like those Jesus criticized. Instead of freely serving others, we can help in order to get something in return. We can oppose immoral political decisions out of hatred rather than love. We can donate to charity only to improve our public image. As T. S. Eliot said, the greatest treason is to do the right thing for the wrong reason.

But get the heart right and good things follow.

Guard your heart above all else,
for it determines the course of your life.

PROVERBS 4:23

How is your heart?

In what area are you most tempted to do the right thing for the wrong reason?

HOLY WORDS

"But I say, if you are even angry with someone, you are subject to judgment!"

MATTHEW 5:22

Some years ago I experienced a dark and prolonged feud with a coworker. "It troubles me to say this," I confessed to a friend, "but sometimes I wish this person was dead." So tormented had I become that I dreamed of my colleague's eradication. My anger at having been wronged had become ugliness of the highest order.

At its best, anger arises from injustice. At its worst, anger becomes murderous in intent. Beyond wanting to see a wrong righted, we find ourselves wishing the destruction of a person, even if only through our words.

To the religious leaders of Jesus' day who follow only the letter of the Ten Commandments (in this case, Exodus 20:13), no sin is committed in anger unless actual murder is the result. Jesus, though, never looks at an action alone but the heart behind it. Trace the swing of the fist, the kick of the boot, the stab of the knife, or the planting of the bomb to its root and you will find hate. And trace that hate back further and you'll find the seed of festered anger. This, Jesus says in his Sermon, is just as bad as murder itself (Matthew 5:22).

The first sign our anger is turning murderous is when we start belittling those we have a problem with. Jesus cracks open two words popular in his day to reveal their vicious spirit. *Raca* was an Aramaic word used to insult someone's intelligence. A modern equivalent might be to call someone an "idiot." And *mōre,* the Greek word for "fool," was an insult to someone's character. Imagine the worst swear words you can think of, applied with a sneer to another person. Can you feel how murderous these words are? Such contempt dehumanizes people, declares them worthless, and seeks their destruction. Jesus warns that using such language will incur the most severe judgment.

We see the truth of Jesus' words everywhere we look—in the schoolyard where cruel names leave lasting scars, on the sports field where players sling racial slurs, in the home where verbally abusive parents belittle their children, on the world stage where warring countries trade insult for bomb. During the horrors of the 1994 Rwandan genocide Hutus were stirred by fanatical leaders to call their Tutsi enemies "cockroaches." Whether it's "*raca*," "idiot," "fool," or "cockroach," followers of Jesus have no use for such words.

All humans—including our enemies—are made in the image of God. And we are to love people, including our enemies (Matthew 5:44). At times anger may be a natural reaction to another's wrongdoing, but anger must not control us (Ephesians 4:26). We will have disagreements. People will hurt us. But we will pursue reconciliation and forgiveness with others rather than curse or belittle them.

A heart that whispers "murder" doesn't yet imitate its Master.

Get rid of all bitterness, rage, anger, harsh words, and slander, as well as all types of evil behavior. Instead, be kind to each other, tenderhearted, forgiving one another, just as God through Christ has forgiven you.

EPHESIANS 4:31–32

Are you prone to swearing at or belittling people?
Is there anyone you need to apologize to?

HOLY RECONCILIATION

"So if you are presenting a sacrifice at the altar in the Temple and you suddenly remember that someone has something against you, leave your sacrifice there at the altar. Go and be reconciled to that person."

MATTHEW 5:23–24

They sit beside each other on a straw mat—he in beige trousers and a white and purple shirt, she in orange-strapped sandals and a blue and yellow dress. They lean against the mud brick wall of a Rwandan house, close to each other. "I participated in the killing of the son of this woman," says François, one of thousands of Hutu men who perpetrated crimes against Tutsis during the 1994 Rwandan genocide. "He killed my child," says Epiphanie, "then he came to ask me pardon."[19]

In the Rwandan genocide the power of murderous words came to full effect. While Tutsis did their share of killing, it was the majority Hutus who killed the most, seeking to exterminate their "cockroach" enemies. With nearly a million deaths and thousands of rapes, the results were cataclysmic. They were for Epiphanie. But now she sits casually with her son's killer. How can this happen?

Through reconciliation—the kind Jesus describes in his Sermon.

This is another common thread in the fabric of Jesus' teaching. He blesses the peacemakers (Matthew 5:9), teaches non-retaliation in conflict (5:38–42), and calls us to forgive those who've wronged us (6:12–15). Jesus wants reconciliation in all our relationships. And at this point in his Sermon he tells us how to respond when we are the offending party.

Jesus gives two practical examples where conflict will naturally arise: in church and in society. If at church we remember we've offended someone, we're to ask that person's forgiveness before we go any further with our religious acts (5:23–24). And if a dispute arises with a neighbor, we're to seek reconciliation before the neighbor takes matters to court (5:25–26). Jesus' directive extends to all of our relationships. When we are the offending party, we must admit our fault, deal with the problem, settle matters before they escalate—in a word, reconcile.

Jesus never says this will be easy. It hasn't been in Rwanda, where reconciliation has required time, training, mediation, and much, much prayer. But if Epiphanie and François can now share a mat after the horrors of genocide, can't that breathe hope into our own fractured family, church, and workplace relationships?

"We share in everything," François says of Epiphanie now. "If she needs some water to drink, I fetch some for her. There is no suspicion between us, whether under sunlight or during the night." As Epiphanie says, "Before, when I had not yet granted him pardon, [François] could not come close to me. I treated him like my enemy. But now, I would rather treat him like my own child."

Reconciliation can turn enemies into sons.

Do all that you can to live in peace with everyone.

ROMANS 12:18

How have you seen God reconcile your relationships?

Is there anyone you need to reconcile with?

HOLY LONGING

So God created human beings in his own image.
In the image of God he created them;
male and female he created them.

GENESIS 1:27

Human beings are mysteriously designed for relationship. Isolate someone in a room and over time they'll become stressed and confused, and their sleep will be disturbed. Brain function and intelligence will be impaired, and their ability to empathize will decrease. The chronically isolated person will become ill more often and have a higher risk of heart disease. In fact, their genes will begin to decay—one researcher likens chronic loneliness to "premature aging."[20] Social connection is a fundamental part of being human. Like flowers without sunlight, we wither without others.

But why are we so relationally wired? Why are food, water, and shelter insufficient to keep us healthy?

Christians believe in a mysterious God. Scripture stresses there is only one God (Deuteronomy 6:4), but also reveals this God is a community of three persons—Father, Son, and Spirit. We see all three members present at Jesus' baptism (Matthew 3:16–17); we are to be baptized in the name of all three (28:19); looking back we may even see all three present in the world's creation—Father directing the process (Genesis 1:1), Spirit hovering over the waters (1:2), and Son as the Word of God through whom creation is spoken into existence (Genesis 1:3–24; John 1:1–4).

If God himself is a community, is it any wonder that when he makes humans in his image, he makes them as relational beings? Male and female unite, the result is a family (Genesis 1:28); the siblings born becoming supports in adversity (Proverbs 17:17). Friends become those who sharpen us morally (27:6, 17). In origin and function we are relational to the core.

No doubt this is why Jesus focuses so much of his Sermon on

relationships and the powerful forces that drive them apart: hateful words, unresolved conflict, lust and divorce, broken promises, endless retaliation, and hypocritical judgment. These things cause isolation, which goes against the nature of the God in whose image we are made.

C. S. Lewis vividly described hell as an ever-expanding universe of empty houses, of people moving further and further away from each other as they perpetually quarrel.[21] Heaven, by comparison, is pictured as a place of harmony—we'll live together without tears or grief because every relationship-breaking force is gone (Revelation 21:3–4).

Heaven isn't here yet, so we can expect to face some tension among ourselves. But we're to pray for heaven's invasion of earth now and live as a glimpse of that heavenly community (Matthew 6:10). Acceptance, patience, and forgiveness will be needed.

We long for this kind of community, and so does the world.

It's what we've been made for.

And all the believers met together in one place and shared everything they had. They sold their property and possessions and shared the money with those in need.

ACTS 2:44–45

How deep are your friendships?

Who do you know who needs a friend?

HOLY IMAGINATION

"But I say, anyone who even looks at a woman with lust has already committed adultery with her in his heart."

MATTHEW 5:28

In his unsettling book *The Johns*, journalist Victor Malarek reveals the motivations of men who buy the services of prostitutes. In most cases, pornography precedes the transaction. The men watch porn, fantasize about the experience they want, then find a woman who will act out what they desire. The deed follows the fantasy.

Two millennia earlier, Jesus revealed the pattern Malarek discovered. In his Sermon, Jesus says actions follow lustful imaginings (Matthew 5:28). And with his emphasis on the heart, that means it's not just "the johns" who fall short.

It isn't wrong to be sexually attracted to another person. A fleeting thought about sex isn't a sin either, and neither are sexual feelings (as Hebrews 4:15 points out, temptation is not sin). God made us sexual beings who long for sexual intimacy. What Jesus condemns here is illicit lust—*purposely* looking at someone other than one's spouse to stimulate and entertain sexual desire.

We've already explored the religion of deeds alone practiced by the legalists of Jesus' day. To their mind one's fantasies can run wild so long as physical adultery doesn't follow. But Jesus teaches a religion of the heart. Adultery starts with a fantasy, making the fantasy itself sin. A lustful look without a touch can still leave a woman feeling objectified, and cause detrimental effects on a man's current or future relationships. And women aren't immune from lustful pursuits either (Proverbs 30:20).

Jesus' remedy to lustful fantasy is both radical and practical. The heart follows the eyes (Job 31:7), so if your eyes are leading you to sin, go blind (Matthew 5:29)! He's using hyperbole to say, "Shut your eyes. Divert them. Take them elsewhere before your heart follows where they're wanting to lead you." Forgo the illicit pleasures of this life for the sake of the next, whether that means avoiding popular but explicit songs, books, TV shows, or films, or removing yourself from the internet when you're most vulnerable.

In an online age, diversion of the eyes is more difficult than ever before. According to research, most children will have seen pornography, due to its easy availability, by the age of twelve. The effects are devastating, leading to addictions, body image problems, human trafficking, and the destruction of relationships.[22] There has never been more help available to sidestep this trap,[23] but perhaps our journey through the Sermon has already revealed the most powerful antidote: community. Sexual sin is isolating, but confession and accountability can bring us back into the light (James 5:16).

Whether male or female, married or single, all of us are called to cultivate holy imaginations. This is one command of Jesus I'm continually checked by. And he keeps reminding me it's a matter of the heart: we are to treat others as people to be valued, not as objects to be used.

"I made a covenant with my eyes
not to look with lust at a young woman."

JOB 31:1

In what situations are your eyes prone to lead your heart astray?

Do you dress, speak, or act in seductive ways,
making holy imagination difficult for others?

HOLY COMMITMENT

"But I say that a man who divorces his wife, unless she has been unfaithful, causes her to commit adultery."

MATTHEW 5:32

A few years ago, I got into the habit of swimming laps three or four mornings a week at my local public pool. The majority of swimmers early in the day were elderly. I'll never forget the nice old dear who'd flash her big white dentures at me before doing six laps nonstop. I could only manage four!

I often witnessed the morning ritual of one particular couple, probably in their eighties. The lady would be in the pool by the time I arrived—in the slow lane, paddling carefully with a kickboard. After that she'd slowly walk some laps. While this routine was in progress, her husband would sit in a chair by the side of the pool. He didn't read the paper or listen to a radio. He'd just watch her. Finally, as the woman completed her last lap, the husband would get up from his chair and hobble to the poolside, holding a towel and a walking stick. The electric chairlift would raise the woman out of the water, then they'd hobble to the changing rooms together. She leaned on his arm while he walked bowlegged beside her.

For this couple all beauty and stamina had gone. What they had now was arthritis, back problems, fading eyesight—and each other.

Have you ever wondered why commitment like that touches us so deeply? It's because humans are made in the image of a commitment-making, promise-keeping Father, "from whom every family in heaven and on earth derives its name" (Ephesians 3:15 NIV). Marriage is designed to reflect God's commitment to us (Psalm 105:8). No wonder then that Jesus says some tough things about divorce.

Divorce is a hot topic in Jesus' day, with two prominent rabbis locked in public debate over the interpretation of one biblical verse, Deuteronomy 24:1. Rabbi Shammai says this verse makes divorce allowable only when sexual immorality is involved. Rabbi Hillel says it allows divorce for any reason at all, even if a wife loses her looks, isn't much of a cook, or her husband gets bored with her.[24] Hillel's argument has become popular with the masses—divorce is relatively acceptable and requires only the writing of a certificate to put into effect.

A piece of paper, that's all it takes? Just write a note and a marriage is over? It's this laxity over divorce that Jesus targets in his Sermon. Marriage makes two people one—in body, in soul, and in the eyes of God—and you can't just write that union off with the stroke of a pen (Matthew 19:6). In what sounds like agreement with Shammai, Jesus says the only ground for divorce is marital unfaithfulness (5:32). But he makes it clear no one should be looking for "grounds" anyway. Marriage is a lifelong commitment between a man and woman. Anything else, he says, is wrong.

If you've been touched by divorce—having lost your marriage, or watched your parents lose theirs, or looked on in despair as it's happened to friends—none of this will surprise you. Marriage joins people together. Divorce rips people apart: the couple involved, their children, their friends and extended family. Jesus rescues marriage from a culture bent on diminishing it, calling us to marriages that are exclusive, lifelong, committed.

Like that old couple who walk each other to the changing rooms.

Like the God who commits himself to us to the very end.

He always stands by his covenant—
the commitment he made to a thousand generations.

PSALM 105:8

How do you feel about Jesus' teaching on marriage?
How can God's commitment to us strengthen
our commitment to each other?

HOLY SINGLENESS

"Some are born as eunuchs, some have been made eunuchs by others, and some choose not to marry for the sake of the Kingdom of Heaven. Let anyone accept this who can."

MATTHEW 19:12

I remember talking with a colleague when the conversation turned to the topic of singleness. "Well, that's me," John said, quieting his voice. "Forty-two years old and still a virgin." There was a note of shame in his words.

I once stayed at a lovely old hotel with classic drapes and sweeping staircases. For breakfast, guests were assigned to large tables, and I ended up eating with a girl in her thirties. "This is a birthday present," Amy said of her stay. I wished her a happy birthday, then asked if anyone was celebrating with her. "No," she said, her face sullen. "I'm here alone."

In 2013, I wrote a book about broken dreams and as a result, readers contact me regularly to share their stories. They tell me about career dreams that never eventuated, or dashed hopes for having children. Many share how they want to marry but remain single, and feel out of place in a couple's world.

Jesus talks about marriage in his Sermon. But he does so as a thirty-year-old single man—one who is no doubt feeling the pressure of his culture to marry. "Any man who has no wife is not a proper man," wrote the first-century rabbi Eleazar. "He who is twenty years of age and is not married spends all his days in sin," states Rabbi Huna in the Talmud.[25] Marriage and children was the expected path of every Jew. And yet the Jesus teaching on those Galilean slopes is walking a much different road. He will never marry. He will never experience sexual pleasure. He will die without producing an heir.

And in the process he will redefine singleness forever.

Through his life and teaching, Jesus raises singleness to a new level. Singleness isn't a curse to be pitied or a condition to be cured, but a status touched by the holy. When God visits earth he comes as a single man. That alone blesses singleness with divine dignity.

But Jesus goes further, presenting singleness as a viable vocational choice "for the sake of the Kingdom of Heaven" (Matthew 19:12). Paul follows suit, elevating singleness to a "gift"—he wishes others would take up singleness because of its unparalleled opportunity for devotion to God (1 Corinthians 7:7, 32–35). Saint Thomas Aquinas described celibacy as "vacancy for God"—a state of being free, open, and available for God's service.[26] Henri Nouwen said celibate singles could play a prophetic role in society. As no human can complete us, God-focused singleness can remind the world that "relationship with God is the beginning, the source, and the goal of all human relationships."[27]

Jesus affirms the importance of marriage in his Sermon. But he doesn't idolize it. Marriage is not the cure for all loneliness; singleness is not some valley to be endured until the pinnacle of marriage is reached. Singleness can be a calling, a gift, and a powerful witness to the world.

So raise your voice loud, John.

Amy, lift up your head.

Your single Lord has plans for you.

> But I wish everyone were single, just as I am. Yet each person has a special gift from God, of one kind or another.
>
> 1 CORINTHIANS 7:7

How is God calling you to be faithful in your current status?

If you would like to be married but aren't, can you devote your singleness to God's use?

Through his life and teaching, Jesus raises **SINGLENESS** to a new level. Singleness ISN'T A CURSE to be pitied or a condition to be cured, but a status touched by the HOLY. When God visits earth he comes as a single man. That alone blesses singleness with DIVINE DIGNITY.

SINGLENESS can be a CALLING, a GIFT, and a powerful witness to the world.

HOLY ALLEGIANCE

"If you want to be my disciple, you must hate everyone else by comparison—your father and mother, wife and children, brothers and sisters—yes, even your own life. Otherwise, you cannot be my disciple."

LUKE 14:26

I was invited to be a guest on a radio show to dialogue with a woman who identified herself as ex-Christian. Rebekah had been raised as a Christian, had attended Bible colleges, and participated in mission trips. But after growing doubts and a series of life events, she had given up her faith. Today she is an active member of the atheist community in her town.

"How did Jesus disappoint you?" I asked Rebekah during the interview. Part of her reply was that she'd begun to question how holy a man Jesus really was. She raised the verse above, Luke 14:26, as an example.

And on a surface reading, why wouldn't she? What kind of holy man tells people to hate their parents, their siblings, their spouse, even their children? We would question the holiness of any religious leader who suggested such a thing today.

But ponder this: the same man who says these words also teaches love for one's neighbor and even one's enemy (Matthew 22:37–40; 5:44). He loves children, raising their status in a society that believes they should be seen but not heard (Mark 10:13–16). In his dying moments, he makes sure his mother will be cared for when he's gone (John 19:26–27). If Jesus is a man of hate, he isn't very good at it.

No, Jesus' talk of "hating" one's family should be understood in the same way as his call to pluck out one's eye or cut off one's hand because of sin. He's using hyperbole and isn't expecting to be taken literally. His deeper message is serious, though.

We don't know the size of the crowd standing before Jesus as he gives his Sermon. We do know the numbers following him are large by the time he says these words about "hating" one's family (Luke 14:25). Jesus isn't concerned about attracting crowds but radically committed followers who will give him complete allegiance. He is heading to a Roman cross and warns that his disciples will face trouble too—so they had better count the cost of following him now (14:27–33).

This is important for us as we seek to live our relationships in a Jesus-shaped way. We are to love our friends and colleagues, our parents and siblings, our girlfriends, boyfriends, spouses, children, uncles, aunts, and the rest of our families. But we give ultimate allegiance to Jesus above all. Jesus will even redefine what "family" means for us, saying its connecting threads now include faith, not just bloodline (Matthew 12:46–50). The church is not just a gathering of individuals, but a new family.

The question for both atheist and believer is whether Jesus' radical demand to place him above all other relationships is warranted. The early Christians thought so. By putting him first, they changed their families . . . and the world.

"This is my commandment: Love each other in the same way I have loved you. There is no greater love than to lay down one's life for one's friends."

JOHN 15:12–13

Is your allegiance to Jesus greater than to your friends, partner, or family?

Who has ultimate emotional authority in your life?

HOLY PROMISES

"Just say a simple, 'Yes, I will,' or 'No, I won't.' Anything beyond this is from the evil one."

MATTHEW 5:37

As an author I've signed a number of contracts. I've asked others to sign them too. What I dislike most about contracts is their endless clauses, spelled out in detailed legal jargon. It's a litigious age and we've all heard of opportunistic folks with well-paid lawyers cashing in with legal loopholes in such documents. So our contracts get longer and longer.

Once I was working on a book of interviews. The legal advice had been to have each interviewee sign a contract confirming their participation in the book. All of them did—except one. "My word is my promise," he emailed back, causing great consternation to my management. But we took him at his word.

Jesus has addressed the way we treat our friends, neighbors, and spouses. Now he talks about our promises, our oaths, our vows. Jesus' Jewish listeners know a vow is a promise made before God, a commitment that has to be fulfilled (Numbers 30:2). Devious souls, however, have devised ingenious ways of slipping through the loopholes of such promises. For them, it all comes down to the formula you use when you make your vow. If you swear "by God's temple" your vow can be broken—but not if you swear by the temple's gold (Matthew 23:16–17). Swear your vow by the gifts on the altar and it's binding, but not if it's sworn by the altar alone (23:18–22). A simple vow can be forgotten, but a vow made to "the LORD" must be kept (5:33). So if you choose your words carefully, you can make a promise you don't really mean to keep.

Jesus will have none of it.

According to him, whether one swears by the temple, the altar, heaven, or earth doesn't matter. Since all of these are God's possessions, *every* vow is made to God anyway (5:34–35). In fact, to Jesus, *any* vow is problematic. "Just say a simple, 'Yes, I will,' or 'No, I won't,'" he says. Anything else is formula-making which allows for promise-breaking.

What does this mean if we're summoned to court and called to swear an oath? Some Christians—through history and today—believe we should politely tell the judge we decline. Others point out that Jesus didn't refuse to speak when he was called on oath by a judge (Matthew 26:63–64). Whatever we decide, Jesus says his people don't need to *offer* vows in the first place, as all their words should be trustworthy.

"My word is my promise," that interviewee told me. He's stayed true to his word. Jesus no doubt is pleased.

Truthful words stand the test of time,
but lies are soon exposed.

PROVERBS 12:19

When are you most tempted to wriggle out of doing something you said you'd do?

Is there anything you've promised to do but haven't carried out?

HOLY RESPONSE

"But I say, do not resist an evil person! If someone slaps you on the right cheek, offer the other cheek also."

MATTHEW 5:39

One night, a couple of youths stole my car. They crashed it, damaging it beyond repair, and I was never compensated for it. In fact, I even paid to have the car towed away from the crash site! I always felt put out by that. By rights, those thieves should've replaced what they stole from me—and paid the cleanup bill.

In global terms, the injustice I suffered was minor. Others have had not just their car taken from them, but their home, health, family, or freedom. Whatever the mistreatment we face, the same question arises: How should we respond?

One option is to get even. The Old Testament allowed for some degree of this, permitting you to demand "eye for eye" and "tooth for tooth" to get back exactly what was taken from you (Exodus 21:23–25). A second option is to give in—to let the perpetrators get away with what they've done. But in his Sermon, Jesus provides a third option, one which is quite ingenious.

Using surprising words, Jesus says, "do not resist an evil person" (Matthew 5:39).[28] At first, his message sounds self-destructive—like we should give in, and let evil win. But through a series of examples he explains further what he means.

In Jesus' day a slap to the cheek wasn't so much assault as *insult*; a humiliating gesture, it was done with the back of a hand to the right cheek. To be sued for your shirt meant you were too poor to pay your bills, so you were now having your very clothes taken from you. And to carry a Roman soldier's pack was a demeaning task demanded of Jews. Jesus uses these experiences to describe a response to injustice that empowers a victim to respond without retaliating:

If you're insulted with a slap, don't slap back *or* accept the denigration—surprise the offender by offering your left cheek too. They won't know what to do, and you'll show that you're above repaying the insult (5:39).

If you're unjustly sued by a greedy person, don't take revenge *or* give in—for their sake and yours, expose their greed by offering them *all* your clothes (5:40)!

And if you're asked to carry a soldier's pack, don't get violent *or* feel inferior—take charge by going even further than expected (5:41).[29]

Jesus isn't saying evil should be rewarded, that self-defense is wrong, or that injustice should be tolerated. What he says is that evil shouldn't be resisted in equally evil ways. When we're insulted, humiliated, or face injustice, don't get even or give in—instead, *get creative*. As the apostle Paul puts it, "Don't let evil conquer you, but conquer evil by doing good" (Romans 12:21).

Jesus' words are radical. Nothing like them has been uttered before by a religious leader. They are counterintuitive, calling forth prayerful, imaginative action toward injustice.

Don't respond to evil by getting even or giving in.

Creatively conquer it with good.

I didn't have the opportunity to meet the youths who stole my car. But I wonder what might've happened if I'd been able to talk to them, discover what was driving their destructive lives, and offer to help them.

Don't let evil conquer you, but conquer evil by doing good.

ROMANS 12:21

Is anyone treating you badly at the moment?

How can you creatively respond in the spirit of Christ?

HOLY GRACE

"But I say, love your enemies! Pray for those who persecute you!"

MATTHEW 5:44

What do you do when someone hates you, verbally attacks you, sends mobs to burn down your church, and makes threatening phone calls to your family? According to Jesus, you love and pray for them. "But that's not practical!" we say. "That kind of person should face the full force of the law and pay for what they've done." Quite possibly. But loving one's enemy can result in a greater victory.

Early in his career as a Ku Klux Klan leader, Johnny Lee Clary met a black man with whom he'd later have much to do: the Reverend Wade Watts. Clary and Watts first met at a radio station debate in Oklahoma. "Hello, Mr. Clary," the reverend said before the debate. "I just want you to know that I love you and Jesus loves you."

The debate was intense, with Clary arguing that whites and blacks should be separated and Reverend Watts refuting each claim from scripture. Afterward, as Clary was leaving, the reverend approached him with a baby in his arms. "Mr. Clary, this is my daughter Tia," he said. "You say you hate all black people, but how can you hate this child?" Clary made a rush for the door, conscious of his heartlessness. "Nothing you do can make me hate you," the reverend called out. "I'm going to love you and pray for you, Mr. Clary, whether you like it or not!"

From that point, Johnny Lee Clary got vicious. Watts' windows were broken and effigies were torched on his lawn. The Klan burned down one of Watts' churches and set fire to another. On one occasion Clary phoned Watts with a threat: "We're coming to get you and this time we mean business." But the reverend kept his promise to love his enemy, responding with disarming humor. "You don't have to come for me," he said. "I'll meet you. How about a nice little restaurant I know out on Highway 270? I'm buying."

Clary's life would later collapse in a mess. He would leave the

Klan, cry out to God, and become a Christian. One day he phoned the reverend to tell him the news, and share his calling to preach. "Have you spoken anywhere yet, son?" Reverend Watts asked. "How about you give me the honor of preaching your very first time in my all-black church?" And that's what happened. Johnny Lee Clary preached in the very church he once tried to burn.[30]

Grace, grace, grace—to Johnny Lee Clary's brutal attacks Reverend Watts returned costly, holy grace. He loved his enemy, he prayed for him.

Very few of us will face opposition as vicious as Wade Watts faced. Our "enemies" will likely be selfish neighbors, nasty colleagues, internet trolls, or those who oppose our political, moral, or religious beliefs. Jesus tells us to love them all and offers three practical ways to do it: by praying for them (Matthew 5:44), by meeting their practical needs the way God does (5:45), and by showing them kindness (5:47). Yes, there may be reason to get the law involved—Reverend Watts' children were escorted to school by authorities. Yes, change may be demanded of them—Watts was an activist for civil rights. But in all our dealings, love is required.

Wade Watts survived his racist enemies' attacks. Martin Luther King Jr. didn't. Johnny Lee Clary changed. Other enemies haven't.

Jesus never says enemy-love will make all things well.

He calls us instead to a love so radical it extends even to our persecutors.

Bless those who persecute you. Don't curse them;
pray that God will bless them.

ROMANS 12:14

How has God been gracious to you?
Which "enemy" is God calling you to bless?

HOLY PROOF

"But I say, love your enemies! Pray for those who persecute you! In that way, you will be acting as true children of your Father in heaven."

MATTHEW 5:44–45

In his book *The Evidence for God*, Loyola University philosopher Paul Moser offers a fascinating case for the existence of God. His basic argument goes like this:

If there is a God, this God would need to be worthy of worship. (We may worship lesser gods like Thor or money, but that doesn't make them *worthy* of worship.) To be worthy of worship, a God would need to be loving—even to the point of loving his enemies. And if there was such a God, this God would want his creatures to love each other too, as love always wants love shared.

Moser then asks if there's evidence for such a God in human experience. As humans clearly have a selfish bent, what accounts for their loving acts toward others? Why does our conscience often feel pricked when we're selfish? How can people like Wade Watts or Martin Luther King Jr. radically love their enemies? Moser suggests these experiences are evidence for the God of Christian belief. And, Moser adds, as we respond to his invitation of relationship, God transforms us into his loving character, proving his existence even more.

The apostle John offers a similar argument. He says God's nature is love and all human love originates from God (1 John 4:7–8). God's love is shown in Jesus, who loved those who never loved him back (4:9–10). God wants us to love each other the way he loves us (4:11). As we do, he shapes us into his loving character (4:17), revealing himself through our lives (4:12).

Jesus declares in his Sermon—long before the apostle John or Paul Moser put their ideas on paper—"Love your enemies! Pray for those who persecute you! In that way, you will be acting as true children of your Father in heaven" (Matthew 5:44–45). Jesus, John, and

Paul Moser have a consistent message: enemy-loving people reveal an enemy-loving God.

This profound philosophical idea challenges believer and nonbeliever alike. To the nonbeliever it posits an experiment: to test if the Christian God exists, surrender yourself to him and see if he makes you more loving. If he does, you have your proof. To the believer it says this: while there's a place for books, debates, and arguments for God's existence, the most powerful proof for God is seen when we love our enemies.

Because enemy-loving children act like their enemy-loving Father.

And this radical enemy-love proves the existence of an enemy-loving God.

> No one has ever seen God. But if we love each other, God lives in us, and his love is brought to full expression in us.
>
> 1 JOHN 4:12

How does God's love reveal the inadequacy of other philosophies? Using Moser's idea, how does Jesus reveal a God worthy of worship?

HOLY INDIFFERENCE

"If you love only those who love you, what reward is there for that? Even corrupt tax collectors do that much."

MATTHEW 5:46

There is an invisible law that pervades the world and goes almost unnoticed. It is the law of reciprocity. Basically put, reciprocity is the notion of mutual exchange or fair return. It is the law behind business, where a fair exchange of goods and services is made between buyer and seller; and international politics, where one country helps out another; and justice, where a person gets what he or she deserves, either in restitution or punishment.

The law of reciprocity is found in the Bible (see Galatians 6:7). Society couldn't function without it. It is, however, limited.

Simply put, what happens when there is no mutual benefit? What happens when a friend or family member can't reciprocate our care, or a poor country has nothing to offer a superpower? What do we do with people who can give little back to society, like those incapacitated by extreme disabilities or mental health problems?

Sometimes we can't repay our debts or contribute our fair share, so the Bible says reciprocity must be tempered by mercy (Deuteronomy 15:1–11; Micah 6:8). But it doesn't stop there. Beyond reciprocity or mercy, Christian faith teaches *agape*. This is the Greek word used to describe undeserved, sacrificial, no-strings-attached love.

God's very nature is *agape* love (1 John 4:8). He gives good things to the deserving *and* the undeserving (Matthew 5:44–45). Like him, we are to give without expecting a return (Luke 10:25–37), and Jesus describes real love as laying down one's life for others (John 15:12–13). What can one gain after doing that?

In his Sermon, when Jesus talks about loving our enemies, it's *agape* love he's describing. We're not only to love those who love us back (Matthew 5:46) or be kind to those who like us (5:47), because everyone does that. Our kind of love is to go deeper.

Beyond loving our husbands, wives, children, or families; beyond being kind to our friends, neighbors, or those who look, talk, vote, or believe like us; Jesus says we're to love those we have no blood link with, be kind to those we've no obligation to, and give to those we'll get no benefit from. When it comes to anticipated reciprocity, we are to evidence a holy indifference.

Good relationships are intrinsically mutual, and business should be fair—reciprocity has its place. But in my darkest, weakest, most fruitless moments I need *agape*. And with God's strength, I want to give it. Beyond business deals and mutual friendship, I want to give without requiring anything in return.

Now, most people would not be willing to die for an upright person, though someone might perhaps be willing to die for a person who is especially good. But God showed his great love for us by sending Christ to die for us while we were still sinners.

ROMANS 5:7–8

How else can you see the law of reciprocity at work in the world? How often do you give without expecting something return?

In my darkest, weakest, most fruitless moments I need *agape*. And with God's strength, I want to give it. I want to give without requiring anything in return.

HOLY PERFECTION

"But you are to be perfect, even as your Father in heaven is perfect."

MATTHEW 5:48

The late director Krzysztof Kieslowski was once interviewing actors for one of his films. During one interview, a young actress described to him how sometimes, when she felt sad, she'd go out on to the streets of Paris to be with people. Kieslowski probed further and unearthed a fascinating story.

Just six years before, the actress had been close to an emotional breakdown. One day she went out on to the street and a few moments later caught sight of the famous French mime Marcel Marceau, who was by that time a very old man. The actress walked past him, then stopped and turned to give him another look. To her surprise, Marceau stopped and turned to look at her too. Then he gave her a big smile lasting several seconds.

"He saved me then," the actress said.

Kieslowski and the actress pondered whether all the performances Marceau had ever done compared to the fact he'd once saved a young actress with his smile.[31]

Jesus summarizes his Sermon so far by saying we are to be perfect just like our heavenly Father is perfect (Matthew 5:48). His words are jarring, as if he's setting a standard we can't attain or commanding us to become something we can't. But as he'll soon teach us about forgiveness (6:12), it's clear he isn't expecting sinless perfection from us yet. In telling us to be perfect, he's up to something else.

Each day you and I are becoming someone, progressing toward an ideal image of ourselves. This image may be shaped by a hero, a fashion designer, an advertiser, or a friend, but the ideal we pursue determines our character. When Jesus calls us to be perfect like our Father, he is giving us the picture of who we're to become. Friends and heroes can give us glimpses of goodness, but only God is perfect. Fashions change; advertisers want our money more than our godliness. We are to become like our Father. He is our ideal. His character is our goal.

Jesus models this for us. As he sits teaching on the mountain he sits as the perfect image of God (Hebrews 1:3). As we see him we see the Father (John 14:9). In Jesus, God has become man, perfection has become a person. Jesus shows us in more detail what a life of perfection looks like. It looks like loving one's enemies and laying down one's life, of course. But it also looks like a multitude of small acts:

- Noticing a single woman in a crowd who needs attention (Mark 5:25–34)
- Touching a leper when no one else will come close (Matthew 8:1–4)
- Playing with children others want to shoo away (Matthew 19:13–15)
- Listening to the beggars others ignore (Mark 10:46–52)

"But you are to be perfect, even as your Father in heaven is perfect," Jesus says. We are to be perfect in love. One day this may demand the greatest cost from us—even our lives. But mostly it will demand small acts of big kindness.

Like God sending sunshine to those who don't deserve it.

Like a mime stopping to smile at a sad stranger in the street.

But now you must be holy in everything you do, just as God who chose you is holy. For the Scriptures say, "You must be holy because I am holy."

1 PETER 1:15–16

Who are you trying to imitate in life?

Who needs your "smile"?

A FRIEND OF SINNERS

"The Son of Man, on the other hand, feasts and drinks, and you say, 'He's a glutton and a drunkard, and a friend of tax collectors and other sinners!'"

LUKE 7:34

I live in Oxford, England. In a small room off one of Oxford University's historic chapels nearby hangs one of the world's most famous paintings of Jesus—Holman Hunt's *The Light of the World*. Based on Revelation 3:20, it depicts Jesus knocking on a wooden door, waiting to be invited in. He has a blond beard and shoulder-length hair, a serene gaze and a halo. He wears a flowing white gown and knocks gently with the back of his hand. The soft light of a lantern gives his face a warm glow.

This is the meek and mild Jesus the world has come to love—a Jesus who began life as a sweet child sleeping quietly in his manger, and grew to become a young rabbi who wandered the hills telling stories. This Jesus is a teacher of love who accepts all without judgment; a comforter of souls, a champion of compassion, a Hallmark-card Jesus who cradles lambs in his arms. We like this Jesus because he's nice, he's safe. Meek and mild Jesus makes few demands of us.

And so it's understandable if we've shuddered a few times during this part of Jesus' Sermon. "Meek and mild Jesus" has been neither meek nor mild. The wanderer of the hills has told us no stories. There have been no lambs on shoulders, no soothing of souls. The teacher of love has made demands. The comforter has disturbed us.

He's told us that hate is as bad as murder, and a swear word could lead to hell; that lust is as bad as adultery, and the grounds for divorce are virtually nil; that we should turn the other cheek, go the extra mile, give to those who rob us, pray for those who persecute us; that oaths are of the devil; that perfection is the goal. In the space of a few minutes Jesus has leveled every heightened notion we've had of ourselves. None of us reaches his standards of goodness. None of us is sinless.

But here's an interesting thing:

Jesus is also known as the "friend of sinners" (Luke 7:34).

He befriends the very people who break his rules.

Jesus' sexual ethics are tougher than the Old Testament's, and yet he's merciful with the divorced and the sexually loose (John 4:17–18; 8:10–11). He demands righteousness greater than the religious elite, yet eats with thieving tax collectors and people of ill repute (Luke 19:5–8; 7:36–50). He stands for peace and reconciliation, yet his disciple Simon belongs to a political party known for its violence (Luke 6:15). He calls for truth-telling and the avoidance of vows, yet accepts Peter who lies about knowing him—who even seals this denial with an oath (Matthew 26:72–74).

Jesus' standards are high, but he hangs around those who don't meet them.

Boy, that's good news.

Because most of us have sworn, hated, lusted, hit back, and some of us have gotten divorced. We've made promises we've never kept, perhaps even lied under oath. We've hated our enemies, not loved them; wanted our persecutors dead, not blessed. We've been greedy, angry, jealous, selfish; we've fallen far short of Jesus' demands.

But he draws near to us still. He embraces us. Changes us. His death for us means nothing if it doesn't mean this. Jesus buried all our sins in a Palestinian grave. Now we are clean, healed, forgiven (Romans 3:23–26).

A resilient life is not built on anger, lust, retaliation, or hate, neither in this life or the next. A resilient life is a Jesus-shaped life, and he lived everything he preached: never ogling with his eyes or dehumanizing with his words, never lashing out or striking back, never making a promise he didn't keep, loving those who hammered nails in his hands, forgiving those who struck his cheek.

He's not meek and mild—he's holy and merciful.

A resilient life calls for both.

Jesus said, "Father, forgive them, for they don't know what they are doing." And the soldiers gambled for his clothes by throwing dice.

LUKE 23:34

Have you ever focused on Jesus' mercy and forgotten his demands?

Do you ever focus on Jesus' demands and forget his mercy?

PART 4

Your Practices

In our day heaven and earth are on tiptoe waiting for the emergence of a Spirit-led, Spirit-intoxicated, Spirit-empowered people. All of creation watches expectantly for the springing up of a disciplined, freely gathered, martyr people who know in this life the life and power of the kingdom of God.

RICHARD FOSTER[32]

"Watch out! Don't do your good deeds publicly, to be admired by others, for you will lose the reward from your Father in heaven. When you give to someone in need, don't do as the hypocrites do—blowing trumpets in the synagogues and streets to call attention to their acts of charity! I tell you the truth, they have received all the reward they will ever get. But when you give to someone in need, don't let your left hand know what your right hand is doing. Give your gifts in private, and your Father, who sees everything, will reward you.

"When you pray, don't be like the hypocrites who love to pray publicly on street corners and in the synagogues where everyone can see them. I tell you the truth, that is all the reward they will ever get. But when you pray, go away by yourself, shut the door behind you, and pray to your Father in private. Then your Father, who sees everything, will reward you.

"When you pray, don't babble on and on as people of other religions do. They think their prayers are answered merely by repeating their words again and again. Don't be like them, for your Father knows exactly what you need even before you ask him! Pray like this:

Our Father in heaven,
  may your name be kept holy.
May your Kingdom come soon.
May your will be done on earth,
  as it is in heaven.
Give us today the food we need,
and forgive us our sins,
  as we have forgiven those who sin against us.
And don't let us yield to temptation,
  but rescue us from the evil one.

"If you forgive those who sin against you, your heavenly Father will forgive you. But if you refuse to forgive others, your Father will not forgive your sins.

"And when you fast, don't make it obvious, as the hypocrites do, for they try to look miserable and disheveled so people will admire them for their fasting. I tell you the truth, that is the only reward they will ever get. But when you fast, comb your hair and wash your face. Then no one will notice that you are fasting, except your Father, who knows what you do in private. And your Father, who sees everything, will reward you.

"Don't store up treasures here on earth, where moths eat them and rust destroys them, and where thieves break in and steal. Store your treasures in heaven, where moths and rust cannot destroy, and thieves do not break in and steal. Wherever your treasure is, there the desires of your heart will also be.

"Your eye is a lamp that provides light for your body. When your eye is good, your whole body is filled with light. But when your eye is bad, your whole body is filled with darkness. And if the light you think you have is actually darkness, how deep that darkness is!

"No one can serve two masters. For you will hate one and love the other; you will be devoted to one and despise the other. You cannot serve both God and money.

"That is why I tell you not to worry about everyday life—whether you have enough food and drink, or enough clothes to wear. Isn't life more than food, and your body more than clothing? Look at the birds. They don't plant or harvest or store food in barns, for your heavenly Father feeds them. And aren't you far more valuable to him than they are? Can all your worries add a single moment to your life?

"And why worry about your clothing? Look at the lilies of the field and how they grow. They don't work or make their clothing, yet Solomon in all his glory was not dressed as beautifully as they are. And if God cares so wonderfully for wildflowers that are here today and thrown into the fire tomorrow, he will certainly care for you. Why do you have so little faith?

"So don't worry about these things, saying, 'What will we

eat? What will we drink? What will we wear?' These things dominate the thoughts of unbelievers, but your heavenly Father already knows all your needs. Seek the Kingdom of God above all else, and live righteously, and he will give you everything you need.

"So don't worry about tomorrow, for tomorrow will bring its own worries. Today's trouble is enough for today.

"Do not judge others, and you will not be judged. For you will be treated as you treat others. The standard you use in judging is the standard by which you will be judged.

"And why worry about a speck in your friend's eye when you have a log in your own? How can you think of saying to your friend, 'Let me help you get rid of that speck in your eye,' when you can't see past the log in your own eye? Hypocrite! First get rid of the log in your own eye; then you will see well enough to deal with the speck in your friend's eye.

"Don't waste what is holy on people who are unholy. Don't throw your pearls to pigs! They will trample the pearls, then turn and attack you."

Matthew 6:1–7:6

WORSHIP THIS WAY

"Watch out! Don't do your good deeds publicly, to be admired by others, for you will lose the reward from your Father in heaven."

MATTHEW 6:1

Heart, heart, heart. Jesus is all about the heart:

- We are to have a heart for God.
- The heart of our calling is a life of salt, light, and love.
- The motives of our heart are as important as the things we do.

And now Jesus addresses the heart of our spirituality.

The timing is perfect. After outlining his radical moral ethic, Jesus explores the practices that help shape us into people who can live it out. He looks at giving, praying, fasting, trusting, and how we handle possessions and correction. Actions like these shape our heart and character. That's why we call them "spiritual practices."

At the heart of all spirituality is worship. And at the heart of all true worship is a love for God which overflows into a love for others. The glistening thread of the law of love must weave through our spiritual practices too. Jesus points this out, along with some corrupting tendencies to avoid.

All our giving, praying, fasting, and trusting is to be centered on God our Father. Jesus will talk a lot about this—about the *who* our practices must focus on. And spirituality isn't just about our benefit alone but the benefit of our neighbor. This is the *why* aspect, which Jesus will show is also vulnerable to hijack. We can give in order to be praised, pray in order to be applauded, fast in order to be congratulated—in short, we can look spiritual in order to be admired.

"Watch out!" Jesus says, introducing this section of the Sermon. "Don't do your good deeds publicly, to be admired by others, for you will lose the reward from your Father in heaven" (Matthew 6:1). This will be a common refrain in what he says next.

Because, while spirituality is popular today, much of it is centered on ourselves. And while good deeds are always welcome in the world, the potential for hypocrisy is never far away. So Jesus now recalibrates our spiritual practices.

At their heart they're an act of worship.

A God-centered worship which inspires love for others.

> And so, dear brothers and sisters, I plead with you to give your bodies to God because of all he has done for you. Let them be a living and holy sacrifice—the kind he will find acceptable. This is truly the way to worship him.
>
> ROMANS 12:1

Who do you most want admiration from?

Do you ever do spiritual things secretly looking for applause?

GIVE THIS WAY

"Give your gifts in private, and your Father, who sees everything, will reward you."

MATTHEW 6:4

The artist Salvador Dalí once said, "I am an exhibitionist. Life is too short to remain unnoticed."[33] The actress Marlene Dietrich once released an album made entirely of the applause recorded at her cabarets, which she frequently played to friends.[34] "I lust after recognition," Garrison Keillor once confessed. "I am desperate to win all the little merit badges and trinkets of my profession. . . ."[35]

We may not go to Dalí's extremes, driving through Paris in a limousine full of cauliflowers to get attention. We may not do a Dietrich, playing recordings of our standing ovations to friends. But a little bit of us must resonate with Keillor's confession, because the desire to be recognized isn't far from any of us. We want people to notice the good things we do. We may even get angry when they don't.

It isn't wrong to be recognized for what we do. A *lust* for recognition is the problem. This is what the ancients called the sin of vanity, and vanity is never uglier than when it's tied to religion.

The crowd Jesus faces on the mountainside already knows the importance of giving to the needy. Along with praying and fasting, it's a practice central to Jewish spirituality. What Jesus addresses is how giving can be distorted by vanity. "When you give to someone in need," he says, "don't do as the hypocrites do—blowing trumpets in the synagogues and streets to call attention to their acts of charity!" (Matthew 6:2). Doing that is to mistake both the *who* and *why* of Jesus-shaped giving—focusing on the world and its applause instead of on God; giving to make ourselves look good instead of helping someone in need. Give like that and the empty applause of the world will be our only reward.

Jesus' remedy for vanity-motivated giving is to starve it at its source. You want your generosity recognized? Then tell no one about it (6:3). You want it publicly applauded? Then keep it a secret (6:4). Jesus isn't saying all our giving should be hidden, as if we must wear dark glasses before helping a beggar on the street. He's already said our good deeds *should* be seen by all (5:14–16). They may be seen by others, but they must never be done for personal applause.

In the third century, there was a group of hermits called the Desert Fathers. Based on these words of Jesus, they added another spiritual practice to the well known trio of prayer, fasting, and giving. They called it the practice of secrecy—purposefully keeping good deeds quiet, trusting the God who sees all to reward them (6:4). The practice goes like this: we keep quiet about our giving, let our lives speak for themselves, and leave God to decide when and if our deeds ever become known.

Tell them to use their money to do good. They
should be rich in good works and generous to those
in need, always being ready to share with others.

1 TIMOTHY 6:18

How do you respond when a church, charity, or individual doesn't acknowledge your contribution?

What gift can you give today that only God will know about?

PRAY THIS WAY . . .

"When you pray, don't be like the hypocrites who love to pray publicly on street corners and in the synagogues where everyone can see them."

MATTHEW 6:5

A few hours walk from where Jesus and his audience gather stands the beautiful city of Sepphoris. In the last few years the governor of Galilee, Herod Antipas, has been turning this hilltop town into a bustling cosmopolitan center of markets, synagogues, public baths, and temples, with paved streets, frescoed walls, and beautiful mosaics. Jesus knows Sepphoris well; his hometown Nazareth is next door. As a carpenter, he's probably even worked there.

The great theater of Sepphoris is a sight. Built like an amphitheater with semicircular rows of cascading seats facing the stage, it can accommodate over three thousand people. Here the public are entertained by the "hypocrites"—the actors—who dress in masks and costumes to perform Greek plays. "When you pray, don't be like the hypocrites," Jesus says (Matthew 6:5), lifting the word from the stage and giving it the meaning we know today. Don't be like the religious actors who fake it, turning prayer into a performance for the applause of the crowd.

We can turn prayer into a performance for other reasons. "When you pray," Jesus adds, "don't babble on and on as people of other religions do" (6:7). Why do they babble? Because of the *who* they pray to. Jupiter, Juno, Minerva, Mars, and even the emperor Caesar himself are all being worshipped by Romans in Jesus' day. And praying to these gods requires getting your words correct, as this decree in honor of Galerius Caesar shows:

> *The emperor Caesar, Galerius, Valerius, Maximanus, Invictus, Augustus, Pontifex Maximus, Germanicus Maximus, Egypticus Maximus, Phoebicus Maximus, Sarmenicus Maximus . . . Holder of tribunical authority for the 20th time, emperor for the 19th, consul for the 8th, Pater Patriae Pro-Consul . . .*[36]

List all the right titles, say all the right words, perform the prayer correctly, or you'll offend the gods. Vanity may turn prayer into performance, but so can fear.

There's nothing wrong with praying in public, whether in a café for a friend, in a church for a congregation, or in a book for others to read. But when the intent of our prayer becomes looking good to others, Jesus says we're to quit the act, take off the mask, step off the stage, and go pray in our rooms (6:6).

And if fear is driving our performance-oriented praying, we can relax by rediscovering who we're praying to. Our God doesn't require careful prayers or endless flattery to bribe him into giving us what we need. Our God doesn't nitpick the words we pray. He's not a fastidious bureaucrat, he cares for us (6:8).

Pray this way, Jesus tells us in his Sermon:

Simply and truthfully to the One who knows you deeply.

"Yahweh! The LORD!
The God of compassion and mercy!
I am slow to anger
and filled with unfailing love and faithfulness."

EXODUS 34:6

Do you ever feel you have to pray a certain way to be heard by God?
How vulnerable are you with God in prayer?

There's nothing wrong with

praying in public. But when the

INTENT OF OUR PRAYER

becomes looking good to others,

Jesus says we're to

QUIT THE ACT,

TAKE OFF THE MASK,

STEP OFF THE STAGE,

and go pray in our rooms.

. . . TO YOUR FATHER

"Pray like this:
Our Father in heaven,
may your name be kept holy."

MATTHEW 6:9

Everyone has a god. That god is whatever we trust in to provide ultimate meaning and security in our lives, whether it's a supernatural being, or money, family, scientific progress, or success. The god we worship sets the course of our lives, determines the things we pray for, and shapes the people we become.

And so Jesus clarifies *who* we're praying to and what this God is like. Our God, he says, looks out for little people (Matthew 5:1–12), loves his enemies (5:43–48), knows every need and secret (6:4, 6, 8, 18), and is generous with his gifts (7:11). This God, Jesus says, is our *Father*.

His choice of words is surprising.

Jesus could have told us to pray to the "Great Redeemer," the "Holy One of Israel," or one of the other commonly used titles for God. Instead he says we can call God *Father.* "Father" means intimacy—a God who cares deeply for his children. "Father" means accessibility—a God not limited to a particular people. But "Father" also carries risks. Some have been badly treated by their fathers and can project those behaviors onto God. Thankfully, Jesus describes God's Fatherhood further.

He does it by telling a story. In this story, a son goes to his father and demands his inheritance early—the equivalent of saying, "Drop dead, Dad—I want your money." The father grants the wish and the son leaves home, money in pocket, for a life of parties. He squanders his wealth, soon finds himself in poverty, realizes he's made a huge mistake, and then longs to return home. The question is whether the door will still be open to him.

The son starts a pilgrimage back to his father, rehearsing an apology with every step. According to Jewish custom, the father should shun the boy then publicly berate him to restore his honor. But this son won't experience that. As he nears the house he finds his father standing by the window, anxiously waiting for his return. And when the father catches a glimpse of the boy, he opens the door wide, races outside, wraps his son in his arms, then throws him a party (Luke 15:11–32).

This is what God is like, Jesus says.

This is the kind of Father you're praying to.

This Father is so good and pure his name is to be treasured more than any other name on earth (Matthew 6:9). "Until that is so," Dallas Willard says, "the human compass will always be pointing in the wrong direction."[37] Until the Father's name is held holy in our hearts, little gods like money, family, and scientific progress will lure us away. But those gods can never love us the way our Father does.

This is the *who* we are to pray to, Jesus says.

Our Father in heaven, the holy one.

So you have not received a spirit that makes you fearful slaves.
Instead, you received God's Spirit when he adopted you as
his own children. Now we call him, "Abba, Father."

ROMANS 8:15

What is your favorite title for God?
How do you feel about calling God "Father"?

. . . FOR HIS KINGDOM

"May your Kingdom come soon.
May your will be done on earth,
as it is in heaven."

MATTHEW 6:10

Long before it had studios, boulevards, and stars on pavements, Hollywood was a valley of fruit trees. In 1885 Daeida Wilcox and her husband bought 160 acres of California land with the aim of creating a new town. But this wouldn't be any old town. Daeida's dream was for Hollywood to be nothing less than a Christian utopia, a taste of God's kingdom on earth—a place free of alcohol, guns, speeding, and those soul-corrupting amusements, bowling alleys! Her dream was soon under construction.

Like all earthly utopias, however, the dream didn't last long. Despite Daeida's wishes, saloons began opening in the town, and the booming 1920s brought both success and vice to Hollywood. When a filmmaker named D. W. Griffith made a movie there in 1910, the seed for the biggest movie industry in history was sown.

Christian Utopia Hollywood is gone, but that doesn't stop modern Hollywood from excelling in its own version of the utopian dream—*the happy ending*. Truman opens the door and finds his freedom; Luke destroys the Death Star and saves the galaxy; Bridget gets her man; Nemo is found! We all know real life isn't so neat, but we lap up the happy ending because it's what each of us longs for—a world where pain is gone, relationships work, justice is done, and life is sweet.

"May your Kingdom come soon," Jesus teaches us to pray. "May your will be done on earth, as it is in heaven" (Matthew 6:10). The story of Hollywood reflects both our desire for this prayer's fulfillment and the difficulty in its becoming a reality.

As Daeida Wilcox found, legislation can't create the kingdom of God. Sin, suffering, and corruption interfere with every effort to build it. God's kingdom starts with his reign in our heart, *then* ripples out into society. And it comes by God's command and not by human effort alone.

But as Jesus sits on the mountain delivering his Sermon, he sits as the king of the kingdom. Wherever he preaches, heals, and releases people from demonic oppression, he announces the kingdom has begun (12:28). Every healing he does points to the day when *all* wounds will be healed. Every exorcism anticipates *all* evil being destroyed. Through his resurrection he'll show what's in store for *all* who make him Lord. The kingdom of God has come in him. The party has started, God's dream has begun.

And Jesus tells us to pray for the kingdom's completion. Christians aren't called to be pleasant teetotalers who attend church on Sundays and toss a few coins to charity each year. We're called to pray and work to see God's kingdom come to earth, to join Jesus in his mission of transforming the world into what it should be.

As Hollywood shows, we hunger for this. All of us long for utopia. The good news is God will one day fulfill this longing with his new creation. Until then, each happy ending we see on the big screen can be a reminder that a new world is on its way—and a prompt to pray for its completion.

> But with eager hope, the creation looks forward to the day when it will join God's children in glorious freedom from death and decay.
>
> ROMANS 8:20–21

How else do you see society longing for heaven?

How will you participate in God's will being done "on earth" today?

. . . ABOUT YOUR NEEDS

"Give us today the food we need. . . ."

MATTHEW 6:11

Humans are made to hunger for things. We've been designed to require food, water, sunlight, and air, sources outside ourselves. Only God is self-sufficient. That's what Moses learned when he saw the burning bush, with flames engulfing the tree but not consuming the leaves. God is his own energy source; we are not. We hunger. We thirst. We have needs.

Jesus now addresses these needs and their fulfillment. "Give us today the food we need," he tells us to pray (Matthew 6:11). We're to take our hungers to God.

It's *today's* food we ask for, not tomorrow's. The people standing before Jesus are humble first-century villagers. They don't have overflowing pantries or refrigerators. They find their food and work each day. As we pray this prayer, we'll learn to live in the present moment too, worrying less about tomorrow and trusting God with today.

We pray for today's *food*. Our marvelously complex bodies hunger for vitamins, proteins, carbohydrates, and minerals, which God has provided in the hills and fields and streams of creation. But we need clothes and shelter as much as food and water. We need work, and sleep, and clean air to breathe. We hunger for meaning, community, companionship, safety. Bring them all to God, Jesus says. Bring him every need.

And we ask for the food *we* need. Jesus expects us to pray communally—in churches, in families, and in solidarity with our neighbors. So we pray for the fulfillment of hunger in all its variety—for empty bellies in poverty, and empty lives in cities; for single mothers struggling to pay their bills, and unemployed fathers struggling to feed their families; for children in urban ghettos lacking education, and for the forgotten, the isolated, and the lonely. Praying for what *we* need means what we have is to be shared. It means what *we* have is partly *theirs*.

Our food may come from the grocer, and before that from the farmer, and before that from the ground—but it ultimately comes from God. The job may come from an employer and the donation from a benefactor, but each is God's gift (James 1:17). As we pray the way Jesus describes, we'll soon grow in gratitude. We'll begin to see God at work in our lives and his unseen hand behind all we receive.

Give us today the food we need, Lord.
And thank you for everything we're about to receive.

Don't worry about anything; instead, pray about everything.
Tell God what you need, and thank him for all he has done.

PHILIPPIANS 4:6

What need do you have *today*?

What kinds of hunger do you think God most wants to meet?

. . . WITH CONFESSION

". . . and forgive us our sins . . ."

MATTHEW 6:12

Some years ago a guy named Frank Warren handed out four hundred blank postcards to strangers on the street, asking them to write a secret, illustrate it, and mail the card back to him. The secrets started arriving in his mailbox. "I haven't spoken to my dad in ten years," read one, "and it kills me every day." "Everyone who knew me before 9/11 now believes I'm dead," read another. "I should have let you go before we all got hurt," wrote someone else. All four hundred cards came back to Warren, followed by thousands more. A trend of confessing one's secrets was birthed.[38]

A number of "online confessionals" have followed since, allowing people to anonymously get sins off their chest. Some of the confessions posted on these websites are fabricated, and many are voyeuristic. But some have the ring of truth about them, like the confession I read of a woman who cheated on her boyfriend: "I'm sorry," she wrote. "I don't believe in a god, but I need to finally tell someone the truth, even if it is just the internet."

Whether it believes in God or not, the human heart longs to confess its guilt. Deep down we know we need forgiveness. King David captured this experience well in one of his songs: "When I refused to confess my sin, my body wasted away, and I groaned all day long. . . . My strength evaporated like water in the summer heat" (Psalm 32:3–4). Sin weighs us down, it saps our energy. But David captured the freedom confession brings too. "Finally, I confessed all my sins to you and stopped trying to hide my guilt. . . . And you forgave me! All my guilt is gone" (32:5). This is what the girl who cheated on her boyfriend hungers for.

As we've seen, reconciliation is a central theme in Jesus' Sermon. When we've wronged someone, we're to seek their forgiveness (Matthew 5:23–24). When someone has wronged us, we're to forgive them

(6:12). All of this is based on God's forgiveness of us. That forgiveness is the heart of the gospel (Acts 2:38), the heart of baptism (1 Peter 3:21), the heart of the Lord's Supper (Matthew 26:28). And as Jesus teaches the mountainside crowd to pray, he makes sure it isn't left out. Just as we ask God for food, we also ask God for forgiveness. To Jesus, confession is as essential to life as eating.

Confessing our wrongs on a postcard or website may be therapeutic, but it doesn't go far enough. The internet doesn't "hear" our confession. A postcard can't "forgive" our sin. The guy who hasn't spoken to his father in a decade is still estranged. The sins of the cheating girlfriend haven't gone away.

"Forgive us our sins . . ." Jesus tells us to pray.

Confess to the One who takes all your sins away.

If we claim we have no sin, we are only fooling ourselves and not living in the truth. But if we confess our sins to him, he is faithful and just to forgive us our sins and to cleanse us from all wickedness.

1 JOHN 1:8–9

Is there any sin weighing heavily on your heart today?

Is there any sin too big for Jesus' sacrifice to cover?

. . . OFFERING FORGIVENESS

". . . as we have forgiven those who sin against us."

MATTHEW 6:12

Someone lies to us, takes advantage of us, or insults one of our friends. Or they betray us, spread rumors about us, or abuse someone we love. We feel hurt, become embittered, and are soon contemplating ways to get even. They should pay for what they've done, we say. They should face justice. What they've done is *wrong*.

Then we hear these words of Jesus in his Sermon. He says we're to ask God to forgive us, "as we have forgiven those who sin against us" (Matthew 6:12). He even says we won't be forgiven by God if we don't forgive others (6:14–15). They're tough words. How then do we truly forgive, especially when the crimes are great?

We can get some help on this from author and minister R. T. Kendall. His book *Total Forgiveness* is a modern classic on the topic. In a radio interview, he gave me these seven helpful steps to forgiving others:[39]

First, tell nobody what they did to you. "The main reason we tell others about the offense is to hurt those who've hurt us," R. T. says. While it may be appropriate to tell someone for therapeutic reasons, or in the event others are in danger, don't get revenge by spreading word about what's been done to you.

Second, don't let them be afraid of you. It's easy to intimidate someone who has hurt you. "We walk into a room, they freeze, and we think, *good*," R. T. says. "But when you set someone free, you refuse to let them be afraid of you."

Third, don't let them feel guilty. Like fear, guilt can be used to punish someone. When we say, "I forgive you, but I hope you feel guilty about it," we are still wanting them to suffer. Instead, "Perfect love drives out fear, because fear has to do with punishment" (1 John 4:18 NIV).

Fourth, let them save face. "Instead of saying 'Gotcha,' you look the other way," R. T. says. When Joseph forgave his brothers for selling him into slavery, he helped them save face by showing that God had been sovereign over the affair (Genesis 50:18–20).

Fifth, protect them from their darkest secret. "You may know something about someone that would destroy them if it were told," R. T. adds. "Total forgiveness is when you're sure nobody will ever know. That's the way Jesus is with us. He protects us from *our* darkest secret."

Sixth, pray for them. "You're asking God to do for them what God has done for you. He's forgiven your sins by Jesus' death on the cross. Now you let them off the hook by asking God to bless them too" (Colossians 3:13).

Seventh, continue to forgive. There will probably be days when the offense comes back to mind. When that happens we have to forgive again, following Jesus' command to forgive as long as there's need (Matthew 18:21–22).

"Totally forgiving another person that has hurt you is the hardest thing in the world anybody ever has to do," R. T. says. "And yet it's right, because we are hurting ourselves when we carry this burden, and it is medically and psychologically emancipating when we set the perpetrator free."

Make allowance for each other's faults, and forgive anyone who offends you. Remember, the Lord forgave you, so you must forgive others.

COLOSSIANS 3:13

Who do you need to forgive today?

Which of these seven steps can you work on?

. . . SEEKING RESCUE

"And don't let us yield to temptation,
but rescue us from the evil one."

MATTHEW 6:13

In her early twenties, Mimi began working at a brothel, lured by the offer of easy money to pay off her university debts. "At first it felt empowering," she told me. "How many people can command a day's wages for half an hour of their time?"[40] But the darkness of this world soon became evident. "I met other sex workers who dreamed of going back to finish their degrees but got hooked on drugs or pimped out instead," she said. "And I always wondered whether my clients were depriving their children of school books or shoes by handing their money to me."

Despite this, Mimi kept working in the field. The big money began funding a lavish lifestyle, and working nights meant she lost touch with her friends. Then things began spiraling out of control.

"I fell pregnant to a client," Mimi said. "I realized I couldn't raise a child in that environment, so I left. I married the father, but he couldn't forget my past so we broke up. I went from having lots of money each week to having little. All my social connections were gone and I felt isolated. That's when I started contemplating suicide."

Instead, Mimi cried out to Jesus. "I asked him to take control of my life and this inner calm came over me like I'd never felt before," she said. "That was only six weeks ago and ever since the depression has gone." But with money tight and her work history difficult to explain to potential employers, Mimi was feeling tempted to return to her old life. "If the options are raising my child on instant noodles or getting good money working at a massage parlor, maybe I'll go back."

Mimi's experience reveals the strategy the evil one, Satan, uses to trap all of us. First, *he exploits our weakness with an enticing proposition*: we're in debt and he offers us money through prostitution or theft; we're lonely and he suggests an affair to find intimacy; we're depressed and he proposes a stimulant to make us happy. Then *he isolates us from the people we need*: we lose touch with friends and family, we drift from Christian community, and we start living in secret to hide our shame. Finally, *he enslaves us*: like Mimi, we find ourselves trapped in a place of destruction.

"And don't let us yield to temptation," Jesus teaches us to pray next in his Sermon, "but rescue us from the evil one" (Matthew 6:13). The prayer recognizes something important about us: our vulnerability. We're vulnerable to our own distorted desires (James 1:13–15), the alluring but destructive ways of the world (1 John 2:15–17), and the strategies of the evil one who plots our downfall (1 Peter 5:8–9).

"Don't let Mimi yield to temptation, Lord!" we pray. "Rescue her from the evil one!"

"And don't let *me* yield to my own temptations!" we pray, whether to lust, get revenge, spread gossip, or give in to some other addictive desire. "Rescue us from the evil one, Lord! Don't let us be enticed, isolated, and enslaved."

Some Bible translations end Jesus' teaching on prayer with the words, "For yours is the kingdom and the power and the glory forever. Amen." While they're not found in the oldest biblical manuscripts we have,[41] the words are a fitting conclusion to our prayers. As we pray for ourselves and others like Mimi, we acknowledge the existence of a greater power than ourselves or the evil one.

We pray to the One who has all power to rescue us.

> The temptations in your life are no different from what others experience. And God is faithful. He will not allow the temptation to be more than you can stand. When you are tempted, he will show you a way out so that you can endure.
>
> 1 CORINTHIANS 10:13

When are you most vulnerable to temptation?
How have you prepared yourself for those moments?

FAST THIS WAY

"But when you fast, comb your hair and wash your face. Then no one will notice that you are fasting, except your Father. . . ."

MATTHEW 6:17–18

I used to think fasting was a kind of spiritual hunger strike, an act of blackmail aimed at God, forcing him to do what we asked. I soon learned otherwise, but must confess that to this point in time, I haven't fasted very often or for very long. In fact, I once sat down to read a book on fasting while eating Nutella out of the jar! My fasting credentials are sketchy, but one experience helped me realize what fasting is all about.

For a short time some years ago, I was the youth minister of a church. I was in over my head, struggling to do a job with gifts I didn't have and getting burned out in the process. I needed some intensive time with God, so I arranged a few days retreat at a friend's cabin in the country.

I drove to the cabin early. I took only a Bible and a journal with me, vowing not to read, watch, or listen to anything else during my time away. On arrival at the cabin I put my clothes in the bedroom and my food in the fridge, then got to praying.

God draws near to us when we seek him (James 4:8). After an hour or so of panicked prayers about the pressures I was facing, a strange calm came over me. My prayers began to drift away from my stresses and focus on God's presence. I started reading scripture, and wrote down some important discoveries. I prayed, praised, read, and wrote for the next few hours, realizing later that I'd skipped lunch. "Maybe this is what fasting is all about," I thought, "focusing on God to the exclusion of all else." I continued the fast the next day, with some difficulty—but returned home a different person.

As with giving and praying, Jesus tells us the *why* behind our fasting is key. Mondays and Thursdays were market days in Jesus' time—prime days for the religious actors to publicize their fasting to the crowds (Matthew 6:16). Instead, love for God, others, and self must drive the practice. We fast primarily out of love for God, making him the focus (6:18). We love others by fasting for their safety (Esther 4:16), during their suffering (Psalm 35:11–16), or in times of national crisis (2 Chronicles 20:1–4). And fasting's personal effects benefit us profoundly too: helping us hear from God (Acts 13:2), be empowered for mission (13:3), become sensitive to the Spirit, and keep our desires in check.

Some people fast from shopping malls to keep consumerism at bay, the apostle Paul talked about sexual fasts between spouses (1 Corinthians 7:5), and I fasted from media while on retreat that time. These all have their place, but in his Sermon Jesus talks about fasting from *food,* only drinking water while praying to the Father. While there are no explicit biblical commands to fast as there are for us to give and to pray, Jesus assumes we'll do all three. Some shouldn't fast for health or body image reasons, but with a little guidance, most of us should give it a try.[42]

Christian fasting isn't about looking good to others, either by losing weight or being praised for our religiosity. And neither is it a hunger strike. Fasting is about focusing on God in prayer, to the exclusion of all else.

I once discovered that by accident.

Now I need to put that discovery further into practice.

"People do not live by bread alone,
but by every word that comes from the mouth of God."

MATTHEW 4:4

Have you ever attempted a fast?
How might God be calling you to practice fasting?

CONSUME THIS WAY

"You cannot serve both God and money."

MATTHEW 6:24

A few years ago a jeans company ran a controversial TV commercial. The ad begins with a woman meeting three men in a dark street at night. She gets into a car and is driven to a secluded river. There she wades into the dark waters, followed by her three friends. The men wear the brand-name jeans; the woman wears a skirt, which she peels off before lowering herself waist-deep into the river. One of the men then wades close, puts his hand on her forehead, and pushes her backward, baptizing her in the water. As the woman comes up, we see a miracle has happened: she now wears the same brand-name jeans as the men. The phrase "Born Again" appears on the screen.[43]

That advertisement makes explicit what is happening in many secular societies. We're seeking salvation at the shopping mall and rebirth through brand names. We're looking for new life through what we own, drive, wear, and buy. That makes materialism a religion and money a god. But worship of this god exacts a toll.

In his book *The Selfish Capitalist*, psychologist Oliver James outlines the effects of materialism on those who practice it. With their emphasis on money, possessions, and personal appearance, materialists suffer increased levels of depression, anxiety, aggression, narcissism, substance abuse, and relationship breakdown.[44] As our devotion to this religion grows, we become less loyal, forgiving, helpful, and joyful, and more cynical, fearful, manipulative, and insecure. James adds that most modern psychiatric disorders are virtually unknown outside westernized societies. A materialistic culture leads to sickness of the deepest kind.

We become like what we worship. As Jesus continues his Sermon he reveals that money and possessions are powerful gods that seek to shape us into their image (Matthew 6:21, 24). Bow to the god of money and your soul will be robbed of light and life (6:22–23). Obsess over material things and you'll become anxious and worried (6:25–32). Our hearts are shaped by what we value most, so make sure heaven himself is your treasure (6:21).

As Oliver James has shown, materialism is a pervasive illness that affects us more than we know. Jesus' remedy for it is timeless: renounce the god of money for the God of love (6:24); rest in your Father's concern for you, trusting him to provide what you need (6:26, 30), and orient your life around his agenda (6:33), finding your purpose in working for things that last (6:20).

Perhaps the best way to rid ourselves of materialism is to increase our level of generosity. When money becomes an idol, we can give more of it away. If our cars, clothes, and "treasures" become too precious, we can share them with others or donate them to those in need. Relinquished gods hold no power over us.

Consume this way, Jesus says in his Sermon:

With a generous spirit and your eyes on the Father.

Tell them to use their money to do good. They should be rich in good works and generous to those in need, always being ready to share with others. By doing this they will be storing up their treasure as a good foundation for the future so that they may experience true life.

1 TIMOTHY 6:18–19

How concerned are you about your public image or status?
How do you seek "salvation" through things other than God?

TRUST THIS WAY

"That is why I tell you not to worry about everyday life—whether you have enough food and drink, or enough clothes to wear."

MATTHEW 6:25

As a child I worried about making friends at school. As a student I worried about getting work after graduation. Over the years I've worried about passing exams, wearing the right clothes, earning enough money, and fitting in. I've worried about bank loans, career paths, and finding someone to marry. Today I worry about the sales of my books and the health of my parents. Since we don't have children, Merryn and I sometimes wonder who will look after us when we're old.

What do you worry about? Make a list. Some of your fears may be similar to mine.

Jesus addresses humanity's most common problems in his Sermon: finding purpose, achieving reconciliation, responding to evil, handling possessions. Now he turns to the pervasive problem of worry, giving us two reasons why we should unlearn the habit.

One reason is practical: to worry is to waste energy on something that may never happen. Look at the list of worries you've made. Notice how many relate to the future—that you won't get the job, get married, or have your project succeed. The fact is we don't know the future. Most things we worry about won't happen, and worrying isn't making an ounce of difference to the ones that will. "Can all your worries add a single moment to your life?" Jesus asks (Matthew 6:27). They can't. "So don't worry about tomorrow," he says. "Today's trouble is enough for today" (6:34).

The other reason is theological: worry is tied to worship. If you hope Minerva or Mars or money will look after you, then good luck. Those gods are incapable of meeting human need, so you're left fending for yourself (6:31–32). But Father God is different, Jesus says. He's real, he cares, he responds. And he's active in your life right now.

To make his point, Jesus leads us through a guided meditation on the natural world. "Look at the birds," he says. Look how God "feeds" them each day (6:26). "Look at the lilies of the field and how they grow," he adds. Look how beautifully "dressed" they are (6:28–29). Look—God is active right now, providing for creation. And this same God is active in your life too. So don't worry about what you'll eat or wear—or anything else that makes you anxious. If God looks after birds and flowers like this, won't he look after you, his child?

Why are we so slow to trust God, Jesus asks (6:30)? Here's my hunch: we subtly forget that God is active in our lives, so we take his burdens on ourselves. But God *is* at work. He's prompting us to pray (Psalm 27:8), making us more like Christ each day (2 Corinthians 3:18), and giving us the desire to do his will (Philippians 2:13). And he's actively providing for our needs.

Jesus isn't saying that anticipating problems or planning ahead is wrong, or that we should stop working because "the Lord will provide." Birds work hard for their food and so should we (2 Thessalonians 3:10–12). Neither is he promising a carefree life (Matthew 6:34). There will be storms, there will be difficulties—but our lives are to be driven by trust, not worry.

So we trust God with today's needs and problems.

And remember our fears about the future may never come true.

Don't worry about anything; instead, pray about everything.
Tell God what you need, and thank him for all he has done.

PHILIPPIANS 4:6

How many of your worries concern the future?
How can you rewrite your list of "worries" into a list of "trusts"?

CORRECT THIS WAY

"Hypocrite! First get rid of the log in your own eye; then you will see well enough to deal with the speck in your friend's eye."

MATTHEW 7:5

The other day I read an interview with an author on a popular website. The author was asked about her divorce, which had been quite public at the time, and her subsequent remarriage. As was appropriate, she kept the details of the divorce private, saying only that it had devastated both her and her ex-husband. She'd believed marriage was a lifelong commitment, and still did—so she sought pastoral guidance as to whether remarriage was even an option for her. She then shared what she'd learned about the importance of Christian community in times of failure.

I finished the article, then scrolled down to the comments section.

The words there were ruthless.

On the basis of that short article, stones were hurled at the author from every direction. "The Bible says divorce is a sin," "Remarriage makes her an adulterer," "She clearly hasn't repented," people said. One person accused her of talking about herself too much. Another said she hadn't shared enough. One charming individual scanned the net for everything he could find on this author, twisting what he found to belittle her life and work. Through those comments the author's personhood was ravaged.

A sea breeze drifts across the mountainside as the crowds await Jesus' next words. He's spoken boldly on sins like hate and lust and breaking up your marriage and empty promises. He's said our morality should be greater than the religious actors with their hypocritical spirituality. What will he say next? "Do not judge others, and you will not be judged. For you will be treated as you treat others" (Matthew 7:1–2).

Given the discussion so far, the time is right for Jesus to set some guidelines on how we correct people who fail. In telling us not to judge, he isn't saying it's inappropriate to discern right and wrong or speak out when needed. That would go against much of what he's already taught. What Jesus opposes is a critical, graceless, fault-finding spirit that claims the right to condemn. Such a right is not ours to have.

God is the only perfect judge of a person's sins. We don't know all the facts, we can't read people's hearts, we can never judge a person's actions or motives from some article on the net. Even if we could, we should never condemn them because we too are sinners (7:3–4), and we could be tempted by the same sin. And the purpose of biblical correction isn't condemnation but guidance back to the right path (Galatians 6:1).

Some use Jesus' words here to avoid any challenge to their lifestyle. "Don't judge me!" they say, putting themselves above question. No, we are to correct each other in the family of faith, and to refuse correction is to be as proud as the person who condemns. But when we correct we must know the person well, check our own lives first, and correct with gentleness, humility, and others' best interests at heart.

The religious actors, the hypocrites, love to judge, as it makes them look superior to others. Such people are blind, Jesus says—they walk around with logs in their eyes (Matthew 7:5). The crowd on the mountain laughs, and gets the point.

The blind judge in each of us must go.

Dear brothers and sisters, if another believer is overcome by some sin, you who are godly should gently and humbly help that person back onto the right path. And be careful not to fall into the same temptation yourself.

GALATIANS 6:1

When are you tempted to be critical of someone?
How do we discern right and wrong without becoming judgmental?

BE CORRECTED THIS WAY

"Don't waste what is holy on people who are unholy. Don't throw your pearls to pigs! They will trample the pearls, then turn and attack you."

MATTHEW 7:6

It happened one night after dinner. Bored with television, I switched on my phone and flicked through my Twitter feed. One of the first tweets I saw caught my attention: "Atheists are so limp-wristed because they have nothing to stand for! #ultimatecowards."

Well, I thought, what a way to win friends for the gospel.

Another tweet followed: "Atheists have no morality. They will hug a tree and murder a baby in its mother's womb! #confused."

The nasty tweets continued, each one spewing a diatribe against the atheist heathen. Sadly, the person responsible for them was a Christian pastor. Since he was a brother in the faith, I decided to say something.

"I'm really struggling with your tweets," I posted. "I don't think they show respect toward atheists." The pastor's reply was quick. "You would!" he shot back. "That explains the state of the British Church—because of your struggle!" He then accused me of being "postmodern" and "soppy." To my knowledge, he knew nothing about me. His judgments were based on my one comment to him.

I sent one more tweet, asking the pastor to consider showing gentleness and respect to unbelievers as 1 Peter 3:15–17 says to do. "I tell you what," he replied, "when you have as many ex-atheists in your church as I do in mine, you can come and show me a more excellent way." Then he stopped following me on Twitter.

Intrigued by the interchange, I scrolled through the pastor's previous tweets. Ironically, a few days earlier he'd posted, "When your first response to correction is to kick back rather than think, you're missing the opportunity for God to give you a big heart and a big life." Sadly, he hadn't lived up to his own words.

"Don't waste what is holy on people who are unholy," Jesus says next in his Sermon. "Don't throw your pearls to pigs! They will trample the pearls, then turn and attack you" (Matthew 7:6). His words are cryptic and seem out of place. What are the pearls and who are these pigs? Scholars have wrestled to understand them.[45]

I think the flow of Jesus' Sermon gives us a clue. Jesus has just taught us how to correct people—not with judgmental condemnation, but with humility and their best interests at heart (7:1–5). His talk about pearls and pigs then continues this topic of correction. As Proverbs 9:7 (NIV) says, "Whoever corrects a mocker invites insults; whoever rebukes the wicked incurs abuse." Some won't accept correction, no matter how humbly it's given. They'll insult you, kick you, trample your "pearls" of advice under their feet. So walk away. Leave them be.

He may not have lived up to his earlier tweets, but that pastor was right—whenever we're corrected we face a choice of whether to kick back or to think. May we be people who think, since accepting correction is the path to godly wisdom.

So don't bother correcting mockers;
they will only hate you.
But correct the wise,
and they will love you.

PROVERBS 9:8

What is your first response to correction—to kick back or to think?
What correction have you resisted, then later been thankful for?

AN AUDIENCE OF ONE

"Then your Father, who sees everything, will reward you."

MATTHEW 6:6

Coram Deo. Christians in the sixteenth century used this simple Latin phrase to capture a profound idea. *Coram Deo* means "before the face of God." It says we live before One who knows us intimately—every thought, act, and breath. And it says we should live accordingly. Living before the face of God means living under his care and authority, with integrity, for his glory.

The idea had far-reaching implications then, as it does now. Coram Deo meant there was no distinction in value between classes. The king and the pauper stood equal before the face of God, neither more important than the other. Coram Deo meant there was no distinction between secular and sacred. The butcher and farmer could work to God's glory as much as the pastor or missionary. And Coram Deo meant there should be no distinction between our private and public lives. Both lie naked before the One who sees all.

Jesus came into the world to open our eyes (Luke 4:18), and that's what he's been doing in this part of his Sermon. He's shown us the idols that dull our sight (Matthew 6:19–22), identified the sin-logs that block our vision (7:5), and taught us to see the unseen God at work in the world around us (6:26–30). Then he's opened our eyes to the Coram Deo life—to see that all our giving, praying, fasting and living is done before a God who "sees everything" (6:4, 8, 18).

The hypocrite doesn't get this. Thinking his heart can be hidden, he puts on a mask and presents himself as something he isn't. But God sees through him and says the act is self-defeating. If we announce our generosity with trumpets, turn our prayers into a performance, and reveal the pious reason why our tummies growl; if we store up our own treasures, seek first our own kingdoms, stockpile our grudges, and pray our own wills be done; if we play the judge and trample correction beneath our feet, we only drive the joists of our flimsy house deeper into a foundation of sand. When troubles come (or when people's clapping stops), our lives will crumble.

Instead, the Coram Deo life leads to integrity, and that integrity leads to resilience. Before the face of God we endeavor to live whole, not divided; to be the same in public as in private; to practice what we preach and be humble when we fall. Before the face of God the *who* of our spirituality becomes the Father, not us—and the *why* becomes love for God and others, not looking good ourselves. Before the face of God we live like Jesus—his loyalties undivided (4:8–10), his prayers rightly focused (14:22–23), his house not built on popularity and applause but on doing the Father's will (26:39). On this foundation, our houses too will stand.

"Most of us, whether we are aware of it or not, do things with an eye to the approval of some audience or other," writes Os Guinness. That audience may be our friends, bosses, peers, or social media followers, but in the Coram Deo life only one audience matters—the "Audience of One."[46]

And so we look to this Audience, and to the smile on his face.

And listen for heaven's applause.

"The LORD bless you
and keep you;
the LORD make his face shine on you
and be gracious to you;
the LORD turn his face toward you
and give you peace."

NUMBERS 6:24–26 NIV

When are you most tempted to seek the applause of others?
How else might a Coram Deo life lead to resilience?

If we announce our GENEROSITY with *trumpets*,

turn our PRAYERS into a *performance*,

and reveal the pious reason why our tummies growl;

if we STORE UP our own *treasures*,

seek first our own kingdoms,

STOCKPILE our *grudges*, and

PRAY our *own* wills be done;

if we play the judge and TRAMPLE CORRECTION beneath

our feet, we only drive the joists of our flimsy house

deeper into a FOUNDATION OF *sand*.

When troubles come, our lives will crumble.

PART 5

Your Choices

As you look at your future, what do you see? Are you caught up in your own dreams for a better future, or are you allowing God to mold and shape your future? Do you trust that your life and future is in God's hands, no matter what that means?

CHRISTINE SINE[47]

"Keep on asking, and you will receive what you ask for. Keep on seeking, and you will find. Keep on knocking, and the door will be opened to you. For everyone who asks, receives. Everyone who seeks, finds. And to everyone who knocks, the door will be opened.

"You parents—if your children ask for a loaf of bread, do you give them a stone instead? Or if they ask for a fish, do you give them a snake? Of course not! So if you sinful people know how to give good gifts to your children, how much more will your heavenly Father give good gifts to those who ask him.

"Do to others whatever you would like them to do to you. This is the essence of all that is taught in the law and the prophets.

"You can enter God's Kingdom only through the narrow gate. The highway to hell is broad, and its gate is wide for the many who choose that way. But the gateway to life is very narrow and the road is difficult, and only a few ever find it.

"Beware of false prophets who come disguised as harmless sheep but are really vicious wolves. You can identify them by their fruit, that is, by the way they act. Can you pick grapes from thornbushes, or figs from thistles? A good tree produces good fruit, and a bad tree produces bad fruit. A good tree can't produce bad fruit, and a bad tree can't produce good fruit. So every tree that does not produce good fruit is chopped down and thrown into the fire. Yes, just as you can identify a tree by its fruit, so you can identify people by their actions.

"Not everyone who calls out to me, 'Lord! Lord!' will enter the Kingdom of Heaven. Only those who actually do the will of my Father in heaven will enter. On judgment day many will say to me, 'Lord! Lord! We prophesied in your name and cast out demons in your name and performed many miracles in your name.' But I will reply, 'I never knew you. Get away from me, you who break God's laws.'"

Matthew 7:7–23

A GUIDING PRAYER

"Keep on asking, and you will receive what you ask for. Keep on seeking, and you will find. Keep on knocking, and the door will be opened to you."

MATTHEW 7:7

When I was young I wanted to be many things—but by the time I reached my teens I'd settled on becoming a nightclub DJ. I saved up and bought some equipment. I learned to mix and scratch and do the other tricks DJs did. I built my music collection, honed my skills, started DJing at some clubs and doing well in competitions. By the time I was nineteen, my giddy DJ dream was starting to come true.

Then I became a Christian and soon knew nightclubs weren't part of God's plans for me. I quit the scene, sold my equipment, and began wondering what God wanted for my life instead. I had no idea. So I began praying for guidance.

I prayed diligently for months. I knew I wanted to serve God, but wasn't sure how. At school I'd been good at art, so I pondered studying graphic design. I had an interest in music production, so I thought about doing that. If I were to go overseas on mission, I prayed to know where. In case God wanted me to serve where I worked, I considered options there too.

The first glimmer of guidance came when I heard about a Christian radio network sharing the love of God overseas. Suddenly my heart beat fast, which was surprising given I'd never had an interest in radio. I prayed about this, but had no voice from heaven or sign in the sky confirming the way forward. Two years of prayer later, I still had no clear direction for my life.

Then I read Jesus' words about asking, seeking, and knocking.

Jesus has invited us into his kingdom, given us a calling, taught us how to love, and shown us what true spirituality looks like. Now in his Sermon he shows us how to make good choices. In a world of options, distractions, temptations, and false guides, we'll need it. And the starting point for such guidance is prayer—expectant, persistent, action-oriented prayer. "For everyone who asks, receives. Everyone who seeks, finds. And to everyone who knocks, the door will be opened" (Matthew 7:8).

That's when it hit me. Life with God requires both prayer *and* action. When Isaac needed a wife, Abraham's servant prayed *and* started to search (Genesis 24). When Nehemiah needed protection, he prayed to God *and* posted a guard (Nehemiah 4:9). When Jesus fed the masses, he prayed *and* handed out bread (Matthew 14:19–20). I had been praying for guidance but waiting in my room for an epiphany. I had prayed but not acted. I had asked but not knocked.

So I did some research, made some calls, wrote some letters, and had some conversations. If that thumping heart was a sign I was to serve God through broadcasting, I'd need to learn about radio, get some formal Bible training, and find the funds to do both. In one of the most memorable guidance experiences of my life, all this came together on one day within weeks of putting action behind my prayer.[48]

Jesus doesn't tell us to ask and then wait. He tells us to ask, then seek and knock—to act. The principle applies for any prayer we offer, and particularly when making key choices for our lives.

As a friend told me once, "God steers a moving ship."

They all made plans to come and fight against Jerusalem
and throw us into confusion. But we prayed to our God and
guarded the city day and night to protect ourselves.

NEHEMIAH 4:8–9

What are you seeking God's guidance for right now?
How are you putting action behind your prayer?

Jesus **DOESN'T** tell us

to ask and then wait.

He tells us to **ASK,**

then **SEEK** and **KNOCK—**

TO ACT.

A GUIDING BOOK

Your word is a lamp to guide my feet
and a light for my path.

PSALM 119:105

I once was talking to a spoken-word artist named Brett. Brett's main performance consists of reciting the entire book of Mark from memory, without props or any supporting aids. Mark's gospel is considered a masterpiece in literary circles and, using the King James Version, Brett delivers its story to mainstream audiences with careful emphasis, colorful inflection, and varying pace. He spoke a couple of his favorite passages to me. It was mesmerizing.

What was most interesting was that when we spoke, Brett was wondering whether "a pastor or priest" should accompany him on his performances. I asked him why. "Well," he said, "I get so many people coming to me after the show asking spiritual questions and looking for guidance, I just don't know what to do with them."

There is just something special about the collection of texts that make up the Christian scriptures. Here are sixty-six books, written by a variety authors over three millennia, yet building to one consistent message. The number of literary genres the Bible includes is staggering: the history of books like Judges, the poetry of Song of Songs, the music of the Psalms, the wisdom of the Proverbs, the justice cries of the prophets, the narratives of the Gospels, the pastoral advice of Paul's letters, the prophecy of Revelation. In form and content, scripture is a treasure of beauty and truth, intrigue and drama, hope and comfort, insight and guidance.

As Jesus sits on the mountain delivering his Sermon, he does so as a scripture-shaped person. His love for scripture began young (Luke 2:46–47). His favorite books are Deuteronomy and the Psalms.[49] When he's tempted, he quotes scripture (Matthew 4:4, 7). When it's abused, he reinterprets it (5:21–48). He recites it as his mission begins and as he's crucified (Luke 4:18–19; Matthew 27:46). When asked about eternal life, he points to it (Luke 10:26). When asked about himself, he leads a study of it (24:27). He's told us he hasn't come to replace but to fulfill it, so Jesus wants us to be shaped by scripture too.

This is key as we seek to make godly choices. Scripture is the record of God's involvement in our world, a sacred revelation of his personality and unfolding plan. It is a guide for our feet, a light for our path, and when hidden within helps us find the will of God (Psalm 119:1–16, 105). As we read scripture, it reads us—exposing the deepest desires of our heart to reshape them (Hebrews 4:12).

As Brett discovered, scripture resonates in a way no other literature does. As he spoke it forth, hungry secular hearts lined up for guidance. So let's read scripture, ponder it, bathe in it, pray it, creatively share it, and allow it to shape us.

Do that and we'll soon hear a Voice speaking through its pages, saying:

"This is the way you should go" (Isaiah 30:21).

Don't copy the behavior and customs of this world, but let God transform you into a new person by changing the way you think. Then you will learn to know God's will for you, which is good and pleasing and perfect.

ROMANS 12:2

How authoritative is scripture in your life, practically?
How important is it in guiding your choices?

A GUIDING PRINCIPLE

"You search the Scriptures because you think they give you eternal life. But the Scriptures point to me!"

JOHN 5:39

Some years ago I had a sobering moment regarding my Christian life. After fifteen years of believing, and a decade of Christian service, I realized I didn't know God very well. Of course I knew God was good and holy and that Jesus died for my sins. God had changed my life profoundly, but did I really know his *character* well—his personality? Not as well as I needed to. And the reason? The Bible. Or more precisely, my approach to it.

During my early ministry years I read the Bible looking for leadership tips. I was working in a church, was in over my head, and was desperately seeking direction on how to lead and serve people. Later, as I started to speak more, I read the Bible looking for Christian living tips. That way I could give inspiring how-to talks on belief and godliness. There was nothing essentially wrong with this. The Bible is a good place to find leadership tips, and it has plenty to say about Christian living. But in my pragmatic pursuit of tips and topics I missed something important: I missed God.

Hypocritical religious leaders—the ones Jesus warns about in his Sermon—make the same mistake but in a more serious way. They rigorously study scripture for its principles and laws but make those laws more important than God himself (John 5:39). Their study hasn't produced love in their hearts (5:42), and they're so consumed with Moses that when he points to the One standing before them, they don't recognize who he is (5:39, 45–46). Interestingly, their problem isn't too little Bible study. Their problem is failing to see the One revealed in its pages.

Scripture is foundational for making wise and godly choices. But it can be misread. The Bible has been used to justify slavery, apartheid, witch hunts and misogyny, racism, war, and consumerism in the name of "prosperity." We can read into scripture what we want and miss what's really there. So how do we best read it?

In his Sermon, Jesus has already given us a guiding principle by telling us *he's* the fulfillment of the scriptures (Matthew 5:17). The Bible is a story, and the story is all about Jesus. So let the scriptures tell us about him, then let his life interpret the scriptures. It's hard to justify racism from the Bible when Jesus' life and teachings guide our study.

So I read scripture differently these days. I no longer ask first what principles I can find in the passage, but rather what it tells me about God, the story he's telling, and who I should become as a result. The Bible isn't a self-help book but a guide to knowing God. First go deeper into him, then find all the principles you need.

Then Jesus took them through the writings of Moses and all the prophets, explaining from all the Scriptures the things concerning himself.

LUKE 24:27

What do you look for when you read the Bible?
How can you avoid making the mistake I made?

A GOD WHO HEARS

"So if you sinful people know how to give good gifts to your children, how much more will your heavenly Father give good gifts to those who ask him."

MATTHEW 7:11

Merryn and I got to know Ali when she joined our Friday night prayer group looking for support during her battle with cancer. She soon became a friend, started praying herself, and began discovering who God is.

Ali's taste in fashion and furnishing was exotic. Her flat was filled with fairies, feathers, crystals, and cheap-but-classy antiques. Browsing an antique shop one day, Ali came across a beautiful old Singer-style sewing machine—the manual kind, mounted on a table with a foot pedal. "God," she prayed, "I'd love something like that for my place."

God is a gift-giving God. He gives us food and joy (Acts 14:15–17), sunshine and rain (Matthew 5:45), forgiveness and eternal life (John 4:10; Romans 6:23), the Holy Spirit and spiritual gifts (Luke 11:13; 1 Corinthians 12). In his Sermon, Jesus compares God the Father to earthly parents. If they—even though they're fallen and selfish—know how to give their children good things, how much more so does God? Jesus wants us to know that as we pray about a choice we have to make, or for a need to be met, our Father hears us.

But still, there's a world of difference between asking God for a need and for an old sewing machine, don't you think? Ali wasn't praying for food, rent money, world peace, or even salvation. Her request was a childlike wish to a God she was just becoming acquainted with. I'm not even sure how serious her prayer was.

A couple of days after her visit to the antique shop, Ali walked out her front door on her way to work and saw a pile of junk by the roadside. She stopped in amazement. There in front of her stood a beautiful old Singer-style sewing machine—the manual kind, mounted on a table with a foot pedal. On it hung a sign that read:

"Perfect condition—please take."

Ali ultimately lost her battle with cancer, but not before discovering a God who hears each prayer we whisper—a God who gives good gifts to his children, and to those on their way to becoming so.

Because he bends down to listen,
I will pray as long as I have breath!

PSALM 116:2

What gifts has God given you over the years?
What does this story remind you about his nature?

A GUIDING VOICE

Your own ears will hear him.
Right behind you a voice will say,
"This is the way you should go,"
whether to the right or to the left.

ISAIAH 30:18–22

During a call-in show one night I explored with my audience the tricky topic of hearing God's voice. "Does God speak directly to people?" I asked. "If so, how does he speak, and how can we be sure it's his voice we're hearing and not our own thoughts or feelings?" Maryanne was the first to call in.

"Fifteen years ago I heard God speak to me," she said, "audibly." That got my attention. "I was in the New Age movement at the time, was desperately lonely, and one day called out to God for help."

"What words did you hear this voice say?" I asked.

"The voice told me to visit a particular church," she said. "And it was the last church I'd ever have thought of visiting." Maryanne then described how she obeyed the voice, visited the church, was introduced to the Bible, and became a Christian.

Curious, I asked, "What did this voice sound like?"

"It sounded strong and authoritative," she said, "but also kind and fatherly."

God doesn't speak to people in an audible way very often. While he did speak audibly to Moses (Exodus 3:4), Paul (Acts 9:4), and once to Peter, James, and John (Matthew 17:1–5), even in scripture the experience seems rare. But doesn't Maryanne's experience ring true to God's character?

Seven centuries before Jesus, Isaiah addressed the Israelites during a time of calamity. They had abandoned God and were now reaping the consequences. Yet God still longed to love them. "He will be gracious if you ask for help," Isaiah told them (Isaiah 30:19). At their earnest cry God would speak, the promise being "Your own ears will hear him" (30:21). As a result they would reject the idols and spiritualities that had led them astray and return to the Father (30:22). Isn't this Maryanne's story? She cried out to God, heard a voice lead her out of spiritual error, and came to the Father through Christ.

God's voice may be heard as thunder (John 12:29), as a thought (Acts 20:22–23), as a whisper (1 Kings 19:12), or as a human voice (1 Samuel 3:4). "I think God primarily speaks to us through the Bible," Maryanne said. "But I will never forget that experience."

The shepherd of our souls who sits on the mountain says we can expect divine guidance when we ask for it (John 10:27). Whichever method he uses, be attentive to the voice's tone. God speaks with a strong, kind, authoritative voice.

"After he has gathered his own flock, he walks ahead of them, and they follow him because they know his voice."

JOHN 10:4

When was the last time you "heard" God's voice?
How do you discern God's voice from your own thoughts and feelings?

A TIMELY WORD

Do not stifle the Holy Spirit. Do not scoff at prophecies, but test everything that is said.

1 THESSALONIANS 5:19–21

Jeff Lucas is a British pastor and author known for his witty sense of humor. One day, after speaking at a conference in California, a woman approached him wanting to talk. She said while listening to him she'd had a "picture" which she believed God wanted her to share.

"When you were preaching tonight," she said, "I saw Jesus."

"You saw Jesus?" Jeff replied, a little dubiously. "What was he doing?" Jeff had heard many "vision" stories before and was frankly skeptical.

"He was laughing, Jeff," she said. "And he was clapping, and dancing. Jesus thinks you're really funny. He enjoys what you do."

Jeff judged the woman to be kind and genuine but probably over-enthusiastic on spiritual matters. He left the conference in California and flew directly to Scotland for another event. After speaking at an evening meeting there, another woman approached him. "I saw a picture tonight," she said, "and I think I have something God wants you to know." Jeff hadn't shared the California woman's words with anyone.

"I saw Jesus while you were speaking," the Scottish woman said. "He was laughing and clapping, because he thinks you're really funny. God wants to soothe you with this news." Jeff now realized these were words he needed to hear.[50]

Like Jeff, many people are skeptical when someone says they have a "word from God" for them. The Christians at Thessalonica seemed skeptical too, as Paul had to remind them not to stifle the Holy Spirit by scoffing at prophetic words spoken on God's behalf (1 Thessalonians 5:19–20). But they weren't to be gullible to every well-meaning wish disguised as "prophecy" either. Paul's advice is wise: "Test everything that is said. Hold on to what is good" (5:21).

How do we test a prophecy? What's said should be true to scripture, and be for our strengthening, encouragement, or comfort, even when corrective (1 Corinthians 14:3, 24). If predictive, it should come true. And, as Jeff experienced, a true message from God will often have an uncanny timeliness about it.

A husband and wife I know were walking in the woods, praying about whether they should go to Vietnam as missionaries. Suddenly, a child with a toy gun jumped out from behind a tree. Pretending to be a soldier, he said, "Anyone for Vietnam?" before running off to his friends. The couple went to Vietnam!

In his Sermon, Jesus encourages us to makes choices through prayerful action, knowing that our Father is ready to guide as we do. God will guide us through scripture, on rare occasions address us directly, and will often speak through someone else's lips. When what's shared honors him and speaks into your need with uncanny timing or clarity, listen carefully. God loves to guide us through others.

To one person the Spirit gives the ability to give wise advice; to another the same Spirit gives a message of special knowledge.

1 CORINTHIANS 12:8

Do you ever scoff at the idea of God speaking specially to people? How do you test a "prophecy" given to you?

A COMFORTING PROMISE

And we know that God causes everything to work together for the good of those who love God and are called according to his purpose for them.

ROMANS 8:28

A woman named Renee once asked me for advice. She and her husband had spent years trying to start a family, but without success. After numerous rounds of IVF treatment and several years waiting to adopt, they were exhausted from the ordeal and considering calling their journey to an end. "How do you give up on a dream without regretting what might have been?" she asked. It was a good question.

As I started to share some advice, I realized something else was lurking behind Renee's question. If I wasn't mistaken, I told her, her real concern could be phrased like this: "If we make the wrong choice, will our lives be ruined?" Renee agreed this was the deeper fear she felt.

This is a fear any of us can feel when making decisions about our future. It isn't uncommon to have "what if" questions haunt us. "What if I enroll in the wrong course?" "What if I choose the wrong career?" "What if I break off the relationship and another love never comes along?" "What if it was the next round of IVF that would have started our family?" We fear our lives will be ruined if we don't make the perfect choice.

It was liberating to share with Renee that this fear doesn't need to dominate our lives. As Jesus will soon say in his Sermon, none of us know the future (Matthew 6:34). We're not meant to. Instead we're called to walk with God, place our future into his hands, live by his heart, listen for his voice, seek the wisdom of others, and make the wisest choice we can. If we end up heading in the wrong direction, he can put us right (Proverbs 3:5–6). If the dream dies before God's time, he can resurrect it (John 11:23–44). Paul says that in this imperfect world, "God causes everything to work together for the good of those who love God" (Romans 8:28). If we love him, God can work even a poor choice into the tapestry of our lives.

God doesn't always guide us in clear or miraculous ways. Even when he does, he dignifies us as free individuals by placing the responsibility of choice into our hands. But everything we do happens within his providence which is weaving even the good and bad into something surprising. This is a comforting promise to rest in.

"Your life will not be over if you choose to end your search for a family," I told Renee after sharing some other suggestions. "Trust God to take you somewhere new, whatever you decide."

If you need wisdom, ask our generous God, and he will give it to you. He will not rebuke you for asking.

JAMES 1:5

How often do "what if" questions haunt your decisions? How can you trust God even when things don't go according to plan?

A CONVICTING SPIRIT

"When the Spirit of truth comes, he will guide you into all truth."

JOHN 16:13

A few years back I spent Christmas Day visiting the local maximum security jail with a group from Prison Fellowship. Our purpose was to let those inside know they hadn't been forgotten on such a family-oriented day. We went from cell block to cell block bringing music, handing out cookies, and trying to encourage inmates with the message that God loved them.

I had been on similar visits before, but on this day something special happened. It was in Block 3 as our group began to sing "Amazing Grace." In previous blocks the streetwise inmates were reluctant to participate, but here almost every prisoner joined in. Some closed their eyes to sing from their hearts. Some began to cry.

One man was particularly moved. Kevin, our leader, walked over, put his arm around the prisoner's shoulders, and heard his story. This guy was on his third sentence, each time on child-abuse charges, and to each charge he had strongly denied any wrongdoing. But now something was changing. He looked at Kevin, with a humbled but resolute face, and declared his new intention. "First thing tomorrow morning," he said, "I'm calling my lawyer. I'm going to tell him I'm admitting guilt." That decision had major ramifications for the man's victims and his future.

We'll face many decisions as we walk through our lives—about colleges and careers, whether to marry, where to live. God will give whatever guidance we need for each. But listen to Jesus' Sermon and you'll find his greater interest lies elsewhere: in the moral choices we'll make. Will we love people or abuse them? Will we condemn or forgive? Will we retaliate or reconcile? Will we hide our sins or confess them? In these moral choices Jesus says, we'll have guidance too.

Some time after giving his Sermon, Jesus will break the news that he'll be leaving this world. But his followers aren't to grieve because the Holy Spirit will take his place (John 16:5–7). This Spirit will fill us with power (Acts 1:8), guide us to truth (John 16:13), and convict our hearts of right and wrong (16:8). As we're filled with the Spirit and stay sensitive to him, we can expect his help when we face moral choices (Galatians 5:25).

I once worked with a woman named Maz who made baked cannelloni you would die for. "You must try my pea and ham soup too," she said one day, pushing a container into my hand. I don't like pea soup but took it home anyway. For the next three days, Maz asked me how I liked her soup—and each day I promised her I'd try it that night. A week later, the soup was still in the fridge, untouched, when Maz approached me again.

"Did you try my pea and ham soup?" she said.

I felt a nudge of caution within, but ignored it and went ahead.

"I did try it," I said to Maz. "It was . . . delicious."

And there it was in an instant—the Spirit's conviction, like pressure in the chest and a knot in the gut. I tried to ignore it all day, but only found peace when I confessed my lie to Maz and received her forgiveness.

The Spirit visited Block 3 of that jail and convicted a man of his crime. The Spirit warned me of my approaching lie and made me confess once I'd said it. This is all an important form of divine guidance. Because sin enslaves both the person and those we sin against, but truth frees and repentance liberates us.

In moral choices, then, attend to the Spirit's prompting.

So I say, let the Holy Spirit guide your lives. Then you won't be doing what your sinful nature craves.

GALATIANS 5:16

How will you attend to the Holy Spirit's prompts when you face a moral choice?

Is there anything the Spirit wants you to confess now?

A GOLDEN RULE

"Do to others whatever you would like them to do to you. This is the essence of all that is taught in the law and the prophets."

MATTHEW 7:12

As we find ourselves faced with a choice, we're given some guidance how to decide. We're to ask and knock in prayerful action, bathe in scripture, listen for God's voice, be attentive to timely encouragements, and pay attention to the Spirit's prompts. Now Jesus gives us one more decision-making tool: we're to listen to our own good desires.

Given how adept most of us are at loving ourselves, Jesus says we can base our love for others on that (Matthew 22:39). Most of us know what we need and how we desire to be treated, so we feed, clothe, and house our bodies well, and we long to be loved, respected, and accepted. Even most self-destructive people know the abuse they inflict isn't what they really need. So Jesus turns humanity's self-care impulse into a brilliantly simple ethic: "Do to others whatever you would like them to do to you" (7:12).

There are some decisions God wants us to make ourselves. The scriptures may not be handy. We may not sense God's voice clearly. But we carry our needs and desires wherever we go. As Jesus says in his Sermon, we can use them as guides in how to treat others, mining our experiences for clues.

Remember your first job, when you were still learning the ropes? What did you need from customers back then? Probably patience and courtesy, not frustration and rudeness. So treat the new girl on the checkout the same way.

You're a manager with responsibilities. What do you need from your workers? Probably honesty, diligence, punctuality, and grace. So become that kind of person to those who manage you.

Remember a time you were in pain. What did you need from people then? Probably not pushy advice or simplistic answers, but their care, prayer, and practical assistance. Let that wisdom guide you as you serve others.

Maybe you once doubted God's existence. What did you need at that time? Probably not an admonishment to repent or some vague reassurance, but help in working through your questions. Offer that kind of help too.

You lost someone close. What did you long for then? Probably not clichés like "God needed another angel" or "You're young enough to marry again," but someone's compassion, tears, and presence. Bring those gifts to the sad and grieving.

You've just struck success. What do you desire now? Not the silence of friends or the jealousy of colleagues, but someone to celebrate with you (Romans 12:15). So when a friend has a win, be the first to shout "Hooray!" It's probably just what they need too.

Jesus wasn't the first to state the Golden Rule. Confucius taught a similar rule earlier and it has parallels in other religions. But Jesus affirms it here as a universal truth, part of the wisdom he's woven into the world (Proverbs 8; John 1:1–4; Colossians 1:16–17). He says the Golden Rule distills all biblical ethics into a sentence. At the heart of it is the practice of empathy—putting ourselves in another's shoes and acting accordingly.

So search your heart, mine your experiences, listen to your good desires, imagine yourself in another's place. They're all rich sources of guidance for choosing rightly.

Be happy with those who are happy, and weep with those who weep.

ROMANS 12:15

How can you apply the Golden Rule to a moral choice you're facing now?

Do you think the Golden Rule can ever fail? If so, how?

Jesus turns humanity's self-care impulse

into a brilliantly simple ethic:

"Do to *others* whatever you would

like them to do to you."

AN OCCASIONAL SILENCE

They were trying to trap him into saying something they could use against him, but Jesus stooped down and wrote in the dust with his finger.

JOHN 8:6

We may celebrate the goodness of God during times of answered prayer and dramatic guidance—as when sewing machines fall from heaven to people like Ali, when we hear the voice of God like Mary-anne, or when we receive the same message from two unconnected people like Jeff did. But sooner or later we must face the silence of God too. Israel did (1 Samuel 3:1). Job did (Job 23:1–9). Asaph did (Psalm 77:1–9). "Do not turn a deaf ear to me," David prayed during his own experience of it (28:1). "Why do you hide when I am in trouble?" (10:1).

The fact is, God *chooses* to keep silent at certain times in our lives. What is he up to during these times? An event in Jesus' life can give us some clues.

We find him in this instance stooped down and staring at the ground. He's not on the mountain this time, but teaching in the temple. He's been so vocal until now. On arrival he'd sat down, spoken about the kingdom of God, and enthralled everyone with his words as usual. But now he is silent. All he does is scribble in the sand.

The people around him aren't so quiet. Some shout at him, "The law of Moses says to stone her. What do you say?" (John 8:5). But Jesus is as silent as the shamed and shivering woman standing half-naked before them all. She is stooped too, in embarrassment. But he just makes his marks in the dust, without saying a word.

Finally Jesus breaks his silence. "All right," he says, answering the demands, "but let the one who has never sinned throw the first stone!" (8:7). Then he looks back down to the ground, wordless once more. Silence, a few words, then he's silent again.

One by one, the gathered crowd drift away, those few words of

Jesus ringing loudly in their ears, until just he and the woman are left. Later he'll be silent again during another tense moment, but that time, he will be the one shamed and shivering. Called before Pilate, he'll remain silent to Pilate's questions until the few words he speaks rip deep into Pilate's soul (19:8–12).

We wonder, What is God doing during his periods of silence? Preparing the answer to our prayers? Maybe. Testing the depth of our devotion? Probably. God's silence has a way of testing whether we want *him* or just his gifts. But Jesus' encounter with the woman caught in adultery shows us this about God's silence: Jesus may not have spoken, but he was there. God's silence doesn't mean his absence. And his lengthy pauses were meant to ensure his audience really heard what he'd already said.

God does break his silence. He ultimately spoke to Israel and to Job (1 Samuel 3:4–10; Job 38). The morning finally dawned for Asaph and for David (Psalm 77:10–20; 28:6–9). We may never know why God remains silent to some of our requests. But his silence can be a prompt to reflect further on what he's already told us.

Turn and answer me, O Lord my God!
Restore the sparkle to my eyes, or I will die.

PSALM 13:3

How do you interpret God's silence in your own life?
What did God last say to you that you need to remember or act on?

A PERILOUS ROAD

"But the gateway to life is very narrow and the road is difficult, and only a few ever find it."

MATTHEW 7:14

We are the Options Generation. We don't face starvation, just the choice of whether to buy a Whopper or a Big Mac. We don't lack clothes, just the time to try on all the styles available to us. We can listen to any music, watch any film, and read any book with the touch of a screen. We can select any lifestyle we want, pick and choose our beliefs, and leave our options open until something better comes along.

So the next words in Jesus' Sermon strike us hard. He doesn't expand our options, he limits them. He calls for a this-or-that choice, not indecision. There are only two paths in life, he says, and we must choose one of them. And the road we take now will determine our future destination (Matthew 7:13–14).

Jesus describes the two roads vividly. One is broad and loud and crowded (7:13), its popularity due to its lack of boundaries. It is the "liberated" path of self-will and selfish ambition, of loose promises and sexual freedom. You can say whatever you want on this path, because it's the path of being "true to me." Doing good is for personal profit, and the treasures collected along the way leave little room for God. The broad road is an easy walk. We let our natural desires lead us.

The other road is narrow, so small most people walk past it (7:14). An insignificant gate opens the way to it. This is the path of God-will and God-ambition (7:21), of firm promises and sexual restriction (5:33–37; 27–32). It is a path of reconciliation, the turning of cheeks, and doing good irrespective of personal gain (5:21–26; 38–48; 6:1–4). It is the path of true spirituality and loving God above possessions (6:5–34). The narrow road is more difficult. It goes against our grain.

The broad road feels liberating at first, but feelings can be deceptive. We shout "I'm free! I'm free!" as we walk its length, but its final stop is destruction (7:13). The narrow road appears constricting at first, but looks too are deceptive. We have shed our baggage to fit through its gate and so walk lighter and freer into eternal life itself (7:14).

Jesus here pinpoints the ultimate choice of our lives. He is the path to eternal life. There is no other way (John 14:6), and we must choose definitively and decisively whether to follow him. This is a Yes or No decision. We can't leave our options open. Jesus has told us enough in his Sermon to let us know what we're getting ourselves into.

Yes, Jesus is talking about heaven and hell here, but not only in future terms. The life and death he speaks of are experienced now, depending on our decision (7:24–27). Choose the narrow road and eternal life enters our lives now. Choose the broad road instead and darkness will descend. Then what is begun today will be completed later as we follow either road to its destination.

The narrow road is difficult, but the broad road is perilous.

A choice must be made to follow Jesus or not.

And the choice must be made now.

"Yes, I am the gate. Those who come in through me will be saved. They will come and go freely and will find good pastures."

JOHN 10:9

Which road have you chosen?

Today, will you follow Jesus even if it's unpopular?

PERILOUS VOICES

"He was a murderer from the beginning. He has always hated the truth, because there is no truth in him."

JOHN 8:44

Browsing through a secondhand store one day I came across Paulo Coelho's book *The Pilgrimage*. It tells the story of Coelho walking the famous Camino de Santiago pilgrimage route between France and Spain on a search for meaning. Being interested in pilgrimage experiences, I bought the book. But I wasn't prepared for what I read.

Coelho is joined on his trek by a guide who gives him advice along the way. "There are basically two spiritual forces on our side," the guide tells Paulo early in his journey, "an angel and a devil. The angel always protects us and is a divine gift. . . . The devil is an angel too, but he is a free, rebellious force." Knowing Coelho and his guide weren't coming from a Christian viewpoint, I wondered where this discussion of spiritual realities would lead.

After acknowledging the devil's craftiness, the guide goes on to tell Coelho that this devil knows a lot about the world and can therefore be a good messenger of information. "The only way to deal with our messenger," he says, "is to accept him as a friend—by listening to his advice and asking for his help when necessary."[51] The book then gave readers directions on how to make contact with their own personal devil.

I didn't read any further.

We need to be clear here: the devil and his demonic companions are not messengers to be befriended but forces to be resisted (James 4:7). The devil is not the possessor of truth but a liar to the core (John 8:44). While he can present himself as benevolent, it's only a disguise (2 Corinthians 11:14). Far from wanting our best, he is out for our death (John 10:10).

Coelho isn't alone in his openness to perilous guidance. An author claiming Christian faith once told me she consulted a spirit medium after her father's death. Distraught at losing him, she wanted confirmation he was in a better place. Others who've dabbled in these things confirm Jesus' warning, though. What starts off harmlessly, we think, gets darker over time until the person involved is enslaved to the spirit and its revelations.

As Jesus speaks to a crowd well acquainted with traveling by foot, he says the broad road is popular, though it ends up perilous. And perilous voices call out to us whichever path we take. We don't have to visit a spirit medium to hear these voices—they may purr with temptation, whisper condemnation, or promise to tell us secrets through all kinds of messengers. But we will ignore them. Following Jesus' example, we'll turn to scripture instead (Matthew 4:1–11), and become so acquainted with his voice that we'll discern it from all others (John 10:14–16).

"And don't let us yield to temptation,
but rescue us from the evil one."

MATTHEW 6:13

What other sources of guidance should we avoid?
What advice are you listening to that is ultimately deceptive?

PERILOUS PROPHETS

"Beware of false prophets who come disguised as harmless sheep but are really vicious wolves."

MATTHEW 7:15

Jesus has mentioned the religious hypocrites who don a mask and put on an act for applause. Now he warns of another group with more sinister intentions. Like the hypocrites, they too wear a disguise. But while the hypocrites long for attention, these imposters devour lives. Hypocrites are pitiful. This other group is dangerous.

Jesus calls them "false prophets" and "vicious wolves" (Matthew 7:15). By dressing up as sheep, they slip into the flock and wait for the opportunity to get what they can. They claim to be Christian leaders, but Jesus doesn't know them (7:23). They may even do miracles, but the Holy Spirit isn't with them (7:22). They claim to speak for God, but they ignore the Father's will (7:21). Jesus tells us how to detect them.

Some of these perilous prophets will teach heresy or give sham predictions (Deuteronomy 13:1–4; 18:21–22), but Jesus says to test them primarily by their actions. Behavior reveals the heart the way a fruit reveals its tree (Matthew 7:16–17). The wolves use the church to get money, sex, or power, and these motives will ultimately show in what they think, say, and do.

There was a faith healer a few years back who garnered wealth and fame for his "supernatural" ability to reveal the names, addresses, and ailments of people at his stadium rallies. It turned out his wife was feeding him information through an earpiece. Many televangelists have lived lavish lifestyles from the donations of sick and lonely people who gave their money in exchange for promised "miracle cures." Child abusers have become Sunday school teachers to get access to their prey. Womanizing cult leaders have manipulated their followers for personal gain. Jesus' warning has proven heartbreakingly necessary. Many wolves have crept into his flock.

The apostle Peter dealt with wolves and noticed certain character traits in them. They twist the gospel and tell lies to get money. They're arrogant, deceptive, and dismissive of authority, and they're prone to lust and adultery. They lure the vulnerable into sin, and they brag and boast about themselves (2 Peter 2:1–18). Beware of such people, Jesus says.

But we should also know who the wolves *aren't*. They are not imperfect leaders. Paul and Barnabas bickered (Acts 15:36–40), Peter required correction (Galatians 2:11–16), and Apollos needed his theology straightened out (Acts 18:24–26). A church leader isn't a false prophet because his or her theology isn't perfect, or even because of a moral mistake. The false prophet is condemned for attacking the sheep and breaking God's law (Matthew 7:21, 23), which Jesus says is to love God and others. The wolves wouldn't abuse the flock if they were people of love.

Christian leaders, pastors, teachers, and prophets are to shepherd God's flock, not use it for their own personal, commercial, or political interests (Acts 20:28–31). And they are first to be people of character, not charisma or success (1 Timothy 3:1–13).

Follow these people, Jesus says in his Sermon.

And steer clear of perilous prophets.

"I am the good shepherd. The good shepherd sacrifices his life for the sheep."

JOHN 10:11

How do you choose which Christian leaders you follow?

How will you test a Christian leader's teaching from now on?

PERILOUS CHOICES

"If you love me, obey my commandments."

JOHN 14:15

The pressure on James and Anne began the moment they discovered they were pregnant with their second child. Living in communist China under its one-child policy, they faced discrimination and financial penalties if they continued with the pregnancy. The message to them was clear. "You need to abort," their government said.

That pressure intensified when medical checks revealed the baby Anne carried had significant heart defects. "You need to abort," said their doctor. In a country where disabled children are routinely abandoned, where health care is limited and little support exists for the disabled, it seemed irrational to do anything else.

Then there was pressure from their family. James and Anne could never afford the cost of raising a child with special needs—and a disabled child would bring stigma to them all. "You need to abort," said the family. In Chinese culture, to go against your parent's wishes is to shame them. James and Anne felt the weight of the decision they had to make.

Their government, their doctor, their family, their culture—few of us know the pressure James and Anne faced over their unborn child. But we too will face difficult choices, whether on life-and-death issues or just the temptations we'll face to live contrary to Jesus' ways. When the challenge comes will we be guided by culture or scripture? While others shout will we obey only one Voice? When the broad road beckons will we choose the narrow path instead?

"We will not abort," James and Anne told their government, doctor, family, and culture. "Even if she is disabled, our daughter is a gift from God and made in his image."

Anne arrived at the hospital to deliver her baby. Nurses suggested aborting the baby even as they wheeled her into the birthing area. But little Chen Yu was carried to term and born safely. James and Anne had seven weeks with her before she died.

James and Anne's brave choice has not gone without effect. Their doctor was so moved by their faith that he used them as an example to his medical students, who saw a couple obey a greater Authority than government, family, or culture. "If every parent treated their children as you did," the doctor said, "we would have a different nation."

It isn't always easy choosing the way of Christ. As Jesus has said in his Sermon, the narrow path can be lonely as we walk against, not with, the crowd. But his call is firm: "If you love me, obey my commandments" (John 14:15). Even when it means disobeying family. Even when the world is against you.

It is through such brave and faithful choices that lives are changed—and even whole nations.

> Be careful to live properly among your unbelieving neighbors. Then even if they accuse you of doing wrong, they will see your honorable behavior, and they will give honor to God when he judges the world.
>
> 1 PETER 2:11–12

How are you feeling cultural pressure to disobey Jesus?
How can you follow James and Anne's example?

A HEART OF COURAGE

"Don't be afraid," he said. "Take courage. I am here!"

MATTHEW 14:27

Think for a moment about the pivotal choices Jesus makes in his life—leaving the splendor of heaven to enter strife-torn earth, staying single for the sake of the kingdom of God, launching a world-changing mission with little practical support, saying No to the devil's offer of prestige and power, saying Yes to the Father's will when it means his death, and accepting a crown of thorns, lashes on his back, and nails in his body when a thousand angels could swoop to his rescue.

Now imagine Jesus choosing differently at each point. Imagine him refusing to be born in a peasant village, choosing to settle down rather than pursue his call, saying No to the Father's will because the cost is too great, or Yes to the devil's offer of worldly power. Imagine no salvation for us, no hope for the world, and all reality dissolving into hell as Jesus takes the devil's bait. It makes you shudder. He may be God in human form but Jesus has a real choice in each case. His courageous decisions change everything.

Courage will be required of us too if we're to make Jesus-shaped, God-honoring, history-influencing choices. It takes courage to obey scripture, listen for God's voice, follow the Spirit's prompts, and choose the narrow road. And so the One who hears (John 14:10), obeys (Luke 4:16–21), follows (Matthew 4:1–25), and chooses bravely (26:42) comes to us and says, "Don't be afraid. Take courage. I am here!" (14:27; 10:28–31; 17:1–7). We too can choose courageously because he is by our side to the end (28:20).

Those who've taken Jesus seriously have changed history. Martin Luther bravely confronts a corrupt church and ends up reforming it. William Wilberforce faces death threats but brings the legal slave trade to an end. Elizabeth Fry transforms England's squalid prisons. Martin Luther King Jr. changes race relations forever. Irena Sendler smuggles Jewish children out of Poland to save them from Hitler's

Holocaust. David Wilkerson takes the gospel to New York's gangs. Jackie Pullinger takes it to Hong Kong's addicts. John Smith takes it to Australia's outlaw bikers. And Christians in North Africa, the Middle East, and other volatile places risk death by carrying it there today. Followers of Jesus have changed the world—and continue to—by making courageous choices in response to the heart, voice, and will of God.

The big idea in all of this is that the Jesus-shaped life leads to resilience. Ignore active prayer and the Golden Rule, choose the broad road instead of the narrow path, lend your ear to perilous voices and prophets, and you will never find resilience. Godly choices lead to strong lives. We harvest what we plant (Galatians 6:7–10).

But by definition, resilience requires opposition. Something can't spring back to shape unless it's first been bent. And both the life of Jesus and the lives of the saints show it is often by following God's narrow way that we attract this hardship (Matthew 5:11). Even then, Jesus offers something no one else can match: resilience not confined to the borders of time. We may pay a high price for following Jesus—maybe the ultimate price—but what is lost in this life will be rewarded in the next (5:12).

So we ask, seek, and knock, knowing God is with us.

And build our lives on courageous choices.

Be on guard. Stand firm in the faith. Be courageous. Be strong.

1 CORINTHIANS 16:13

Would you describe yourself as naturally bold or naturally timid? How does Jesus' promise to be with us to the end embolden you?

PART 6

Your Resilient Life

All sorrows can be borne if you can put them into a story.

ISAK DINESEN[52]

"Anyone who listens to my teaching and follows it is wise, like a person who builds a house on solid rock. Though the rain comes in torrents and the floodwaters rise and the winds beat against that house, it won't collapse because it is built on bedrock. But anyone who hears my teaching and doesn't obey it is foolish, like a person who builds a house on sand. When the rains and floods come and the winds beat against that house, it will collapse with a mighty crash."

When Jesus had finished saying these things, the crowds were amazed at his teaching, for he taught with real authority—quite unlike their teachers of religious law.

Matthew 7:24–29

FROM WORDS TO DEEDS

"Anyone who listens to my teaching and follows it is wise, like a person who builds a house on solid rock."

MATTHEW 7:24

In recent years researchers have begun exploring the factors that lead to human resilience. After physical, emotional, or spiritual trauma, what helps someone bounce back rather than collapse? Findings suggest there are four main factors.

The first factor is emotional fitness, the ability to amplify positive emotions like peace, gratitude, hope, or love, while managing negative ones like bitterness, sadness, or anger. The second is family fitness, having strong marriages and relationships by building trust, managing conflict, and extending forgiveness. The third is social fitness, having good friendships and work relations by developing empathy and emotional intelligence. And the fourth is spiritual fitness, defined as a sense of meaning and purpose from serving something greater than ourselves.[53]

It doesn't take much to see that Jesus' Sermon strengthens us in all four of these areas. We're strengthened emotionally by being the "blessed" ones comforted in our mourning, cared for by the Father, given hope for the future, and equipped to manage anger and worry. We're strengthened relationally by living lives of faithfulness, forgiveness, honesty, and grace. We're strengthened socially by living out the Golden Rule, the finest way to develop empathy. And we're strengthened spiritually by serving One who is greater than all, who gives us a mission to be salt, light, and love in the world.

But here's the thing: we don't develop resilience only by hearing or reading about it. We develop resilience through action. Having discovered the factors that lead to it, we put them into practice and develop our fitness. Now Jesus says the same:

It's not enough to listen to his teaching, or even to believe that it's true.

We must put it into practice (7:24–27).

Most Christians today have unprecedented opportunity to hear Jesus' words. We can walk down the street and find a church, or download hours and hours of our favorite preacher's sermons. We can read the Bible in our own language, in several different versions; buy it in softcover, red-letter, or slimline editions; hear it recorded or view it dramatized. We can watch Christian TV, listen to Christian radio, read Christian blogs, download Christian music, and buy calendars, T-shirts, coffee mugs, and fridge magnets adorned with Bible verses so we can be immersed in the Word. But Jesus says it all amounts to nothing unless we act on what we've heard.

Resilience is proven in a time of trial. When the rain comes in torrents and the floodwaters rise and the winds beat against us, do we bounce back or collapse? The rains will surely come—storms of loss, betrayal, illness, tragedy, assaults on our faith, or just plain difficulty—and the time to develop strength is before the first drops fall. Jesus says those who listen but don't act on his words build their lives on sand. Failing to dig a proper foundation, they'll ultimately find trouble. But those who get to work living out Jesus' words build a base for their lives that withstands the fiercest winds (7:26–27).

For many of us, listening to another sermon or reading another Christian book is the last thing we need to do. Pause the podcast. Close the book (even this one). Go. Act. Turn Jesus' words into deeds. Do what the Sermon is calling you to do.

> But don't just listen to God's word. You must do what it says. Otherwise, you are only fooling yourselves.
>
> JAMES 1:22

Do you think of "belief" only as knowledge, rather than action? What part of Jesus' teaching have you avoided putting into practice?

FROM PAIN TO STRENGTH

"Though the rain comes in torrents and the floodwaters rise and the winds beat against that house, it won't collapse because it is built on bedrock."

MATTHEW 7:25

"Our lives began to fall apart when my daughter took her life," a woman told me during a conference break. "And then our second daughter began to self-harm. After several months we discovered why: while my husband and I were missionaries in Africa, two of our three children were sexually abused at a mission-run school. We had given our lives to serve God. Weren't we following his will? Why didn't he protect us?"

Later that day a man told me his story. "My wife and I adopted two children from the Philippines, and we've now discovered one has autism. He gets violent and screams his hatred at my wife. Our marriage is under pressure because we disagree on how to deal with him. Weren't we being faithful, looking after orphans?" he asked. "What did we do to deserve a child that kicks in our walls?"

I heard similar stories from others at that conference—people who had given their all to serve God, then faced some of the toughest trials imaginable. They wondered why things had gone wrong.

Jesus is no slick motivational speaker selling seven–step happiness formulas with the wink of an eye. He tells us straight that we will face trouble (John 16:33). While our houses may stand, we won't be spared a battering from the winds (Matthew 7:25–27). Tough times will come. They did for him.

Jesus is still popular as he gives his Sermon on the mountain. Soon, however, things will change. He will be hunted from town to town (Luke 13:31). His finance manager will embezzle his funds (John 12:4–6). A plot will be hatched to take his life (11:47–53), a plot which will ultimately succeed—with some of the same people now marveling at his words then shouting for his death and hanging him on a tree. Jesus will give his all to follow the Father. He will be perfectly in God's will. And the result? Torrents, floods, winds—trouble. But trouble followed by a mighty resurrection.

"I hold on to two of Jesus' promises," the man with the violent child went on to say. "He promised to be with us to the end of the age, and to wipe every tear from our eye" (Matthew 28:20; Revelation 21:4). Jesus' presence and his hope were what kept this man going. Reflecting on his words and those of others I'd heard that day, I realized something: each person had faced tremendous pain and had questioned God over it, but each was still serving God in profound ways, often with a deep wisdom born from their trials.

Their houses were battered, but each stood strong.

Each one scarred, but each one resilient.

"I have told you all this so that you may have peace in me. Here on earth you will have many trials and sorrows. But take heart, because I have overcome the world."

JOHN 16:33

What helps you get through tough times?

How can those two promises of Jesus strengthen you today?

Jesus is no **SLICK MOTIVATIONAL SPEAKER** selling seven–step happiness formulas with the wink of an eye. He tells us straight that **WE WILL FACE TROUBLE**. Tough times will come. They did for him. *Jesus* will give his all to follow the Father. He will be **PERFECTLY IN GOD'S WILL**. And the result? Torrents, floods, winds—trouble. But trouble followed by a **MIGHTY RESURRECTION**.

FROM SUFFERING TO SERVICE

When Jesus saw his mother standing there beside the disciple he loved, he said to her, "Dear woman, here is your son."

JOHN 19:26

Merryn and I have faced some of life's battering winds ourselves. The fiercest so far occurred while we attempted to start a family. After what became a decade-long journey—trying everything from special diets, healing prayer, and in vitro fertilization to an agonizing two-year wait on an Australian adoption list—we finally brought our dream of parenting to an end and moved to England to start our lives again.

"How are you doing now?" my friend Adrian asked a few months later as we walked in a park.

"On the whole, we're doing okay," I said. "Merryn has a good job now and doesn't cry about the past as much. I guess we're trying to focus on the upside of being childless and the opportunities it brings. You know, like having the freedom to travel."

"'I understand that," Adrian said, "but that will only take you so far." We walked a little further before he explained what he meant.

"Think about Jesus hanging on the cross," he said. "The crucifixion was a dark, barbaric event. There was no 'upside' to it. And Jesus never tried to find one. Instead, he did something else entirely. Sheridan, have you ever noticed how many people Jesus ministered to while he hung on the cross? He ministered to his mother. . . ."

"You mean, putting her in John's care?" I said (John 19:26–27).

"That's right. And he ministered to the thief crucified next to him (Luke 23:39–43), and to the people who crucified him (23:33–34). By his attitude and behavior he ministered to the Roman officer who came to believe in him (23:47), and he ministered to us—forgiving our sins through his sacrifice. All of this was done in the middle of Jesus' suffering, before things came good at his resurrection."

I hadn't seen it that way before.

"There may be some benefits in you and Merryn being childless,"

Adrian said, "but other times you'll find it difficult and lonely. But if you follow Jesus' example, out of your suffering will come opportunities to serve people in ways you otherwise never could have."

Adrian's wisdom would be quick to bear fruit. Based on his words, I would write Merryn's and my story into a book which would later help others start again after their own broken dreams.[54] Our suffering would begin to be redeemed.

"For Jesus, crucifixion was a mission field," Adrian said, wrapping up our walk in the park. "And with him, the fruit of our suffering can be service to others too."

> He comforts us in all our troubles so that we can comfort others. When they are troubled, we will be able to give them the same comfort God has given us.
>
> 2 CORINTHIANS 1:4

How has an experience of pain helped you develop empathy for others?

How else can suffering be turned into service?

FROM WEAKNESS TO POWER

"It was not because of his sins or his parents' sins," Jesus answered. "This happened so the power of God could be seen in him."

JOHN 9:3

On December 4, 1982, a little boy named Nicholas Vujicic was born into the world. As he grew, Nick learned to brush his teeth, comb his hair, and dress himself each morning. Like other boys he learned to swim, fish, and play soccer. But there has always been one big difference between Nick and those around him. Nick was born with the rare tetra-amelia disorder—he has no arms or legs.

As you'd imagine, Nick's life has had its share of pain. His defects were a shock to his parents and their church. How could God have allowed this? Nick was teased at school and at the tender age of eight tried to drown himself in a bathtub. He prayed every day to a God of miracles but never woke up with limbs.

Nick's turning point came through reading a story about Jesus. Out with his disciples one day, Jesus comes across a blind man (John 9:1–9). Since the man has been blind from birth the disciples ponder the cause. "Was it because of his own sins or his parents' sins?" they wonder (9:2). According to the wisdom of the time, there is no suffering without sin—a disease like blindness is caused by a parent's sins or the sins of the blind people themselves, perhaps even in their mothers' womb. Jesus says neither is the case here. This man has been born blind, he says, "so the power of God could be seen in him" (9:3). "Those verses changed my life forever," Nick told me. Now he saw his disability could be used by God.[55]

As Jesus says in his Sermon, the storms of life will come—and sometimes those storms will be chronic problems that beset us for years, maybe even for life. But the God who chooses tiny tribes to bless the world (Deuteronomy 7:7), fells mighty giants through a child's arm (1 Samuel 17:50), comes for the small and powerless (Luke 1:52), makes the greatest of the least (Matthew 19:30), and enlists humble "little" people as his agents of change, turns things upside down and inside out by making our limitations the arena for his strength. As he told the apostle Paul, weakness is where his power works best (2 Corinthians 12:9).

For the man born blind, the power of God was seen in the miraculous restoration of his sight (John 9:11). For Nick Vujicic, it's seen in the people changed through his life. Today he takes to podiums around the world, speaking at conferences and sharing his faith. Many thousands have given their lives to Jesus as a result.

So we turn Jesus' words into deeds, turn our suffering into service, and watch him use our weakness to display his power. "When God doesn't give you a miracle," Nick says, "you are a miracle of God for someone else."

Three different times I begged the Lord to take it away. Each time he said, "My grace is all you need. My power works best in weakness."

2 CORINTHIANS 12:8–9

What is the "disability" you long for God to take away?
How might the power of God be revealed though it?

LIVING IN HOPE

Jesus responded, "Why are you afraid? You have so little faith!" Then he got up and rebuked the wind and waves, and suddenly there was a great calm.

MATTHEW 8:26

In January 2010, Haiti was hit by an earthquake of such magnitude that it leveled around 250,000 homes and 30,000 other buildings and killed as many as 300,000 people. Even more lives were lost as a cholera epidemic swept the country a few months later. Philosophers have a name for this kind of devastation. They call it *natural evil*. With its earthquakes, famines, diseases and afflictions, the world can be a hostile place to live.

I visited Haiti a couple of years before the earthquake. There I met many teenage "restaveks"—domestic servants—who were treated as slaves. They were overworked by their owners and often beaten when they were too exhausted to complete their chores. This is called *moral evil*—evil arising from the human heart. We know all too well how much moral evil infects the world.

While I was in Haiti, a pastor told me about the effects of voodoo on its worshippers. As voodoo participants invite spirits to possess them, they go into a trance, often change personalities, and may cut themselves or do other violent acts. We might call this *demonic evil*—evil sourced in the dark spiritual realm.

Now here's the good news: Jesus came to defeat all three forms of evil in the world! In fact, we'll soon see him do it.

After his Sermon, Jesus will walk down the mountainside to the small fishing village of Capernaum. On the way down he'll heal a leprous man, a Roman officer's servant, and Peter's mother-in-law before boarding a boat, getting caught in a storm, and calming the waves with a simple command (Matthew 8:1–15; 23–27). Within the day he'll have demonstrated his power over natural evil many times.

Jesus has already combated moral evil through his Sermon.

His call to live lives of love and service will turn around cheats like Zacchaeus (Luke 19:1–10). And now Jesus reframes contemporary morality by touching the leper and answering the Roman officer's request—accepting the "unclean" people good Jews are supposed to reject.

And when his boat reaches the other side of the Lake of Galilee, Jesus meets demonic evil up close through two afflicted men (Matthew 8:28–34). They are violent, self-destructive, and impossible to restrain (Mark 5:4–5), but Jesus frees them with a word.

Life's torrents and storms will not always be with us. The One who calms waves with a word and winds by command will one day bring harmony to his creation and full restoration to our lives. Until then we live in hope. He continues his work through us and will one day return in person to complete it.

It is just a matter of time.

We should live in this evil world with wisdom, righteousness, and devotion to God, while we look forward with hope to that wonderful day when the glory of our great God and Savior, Jesus Christ, will be revealed.

TITUS 2:12–13

How have you seen Jesus eradicate evil in your life?

Why do you think he waits to return?

SHARING HOPE

Surely you remember that I was sick when
I first brought you the Good News.

GALATIANS 4:13

A missionary once told me a fascinating story. He was serving in Estonia and saw many deaf Estonians become followers of Jesus. Having come to believe in a miracle-working God, these deaf Christians prayed fervently for their healing. And God did miraculously restore the hearing of two of them. But the miracle carried an unexpected consequence. "Immediately afterward, the two who were healed found themselves outside the deaf community," the missionary said. "That's when the others realized their deafness was a gift which enabled them to reach a segment of society no one else could."

The apostle Paul had a similar experience. It seems he was never planning to visit the Roman province of Galatia during his early missionary journeys. An illness forced him there (Galatians 4:13). Whether it was his "thorn in the flesh" (2 Corinthians 12:7), an illness like malaria he may have contracted at Pamphylia (Acts 13:13), or an eye problem (see Galatians 4:15) we don't know. But Paul sought a different climate, wound up in Galatia and, even though he was ill, started talking about God. Ironically, the Holy Spirit performed miracles through this sick man and the Galatian church was born (3:2–5). It may never have happened without Paul's illness.

The wonder-working, evil-eradicating Jesus is on the move, performing miracles today just as we see him doing before and after his Sermon. As a result, we can expect him to do the surprising when we pray. But as Nick Vujicic, the Estonian Christians, and the apostle Paul discovered, sometimes God withholds miracles to position us to share our hope with others.

I once asked my social media friends how they'd seen God work like that and heard this story from a woman named Virginia. Fifteen years earlier, she had struggled with an eating disorder after a difficult break-up. At her worst point she ended up in the hospital, weighing just eighty pounds (thirty-six kilograms). There she met another girl—the sickest patient in the ward, weighing a mere fifty-five pounds (twenty-five kilograms)—who scribbled a Bible verse on a piece of paper and handed it to her: "For I can do everything through Christ, who gives me strength" (Philippians 4:13). Virginia became a Christian, got healthy, got married, and had a family. And she credits it all to the witness of that ill but faithful girl who was uniquely positioned to reach her.

One day God will rid the world of illness. In the meantime he can use it for good, turning our infirmity into opportunities to share our hope with those who need it.

For our present troubles are small and won't last very long. Yet they produce for us a glory that vastly outweighs them and will last forever!

2 CORINTHIANS 4:17

How have you seen God turn illness around for good?

How are Paul, the Estonian Christians, and Virginia's friend examples to follow when we are sick?

GLIMPSING THE FUTURE

But in fact, Christ has been raised from the dead. He is the first of a great harvest of all who have died.

1 CORINTHIANS 15:20

Miracles can be hard for the modern mind to accept. Science's discovery of nature's laws makes an intervening God somehow less believable. Medicine, not prayer, is what's believed to cure people's bodies these days. Coincidence, not Providence, gets the credit when our needs are mysteriously met. In a secular world we surmise that missing limbs don't grow back, lost sight doesn't return, and dead men don't return to life. Or do they?

In October 2008 Dr. Sean George, a medical specialist, was driving from Esperance to Kalgoorlie in the West Australian goldfields when he started feeling chest pain. He called his wife, Sherry, to let her know, then drove himself to the nearest clinic. Fifteen minutes later, he was dead. Fifty-five minutes of CPR and electric shock therapy couldn't bring Sean back. His death was called when Sherry arrived.

Walking into the room, Sherry nearly collapsed in shock seeing her husband lying motionless with a flat line on the ECG monitor. "Sherry, I'm very sorry but Sean is gone," the emergency physician told her. "I'll give you the last two minutes to say goodbye." Sherry walked to the table, picked up Sean's cold hand and in desperation prayed, "Lord, Sean is only thirty-nine years old. I am only thirty-eight. We have a ten year old boy. I need a miracle."

At that moment the medical staff report Sean's lifeless body took a deep breath and his heartbeat returned on the monitor. Medical equipment readings confirm the claim. Sean told me his miracle story as a completely well man.[56]

Skepticism about the miraculous goes way back. The apostle Paul confronted the Corinthians' cynicism about resurrection (1 Corinthians 15:12). He reminds them that Jesus' bodily resurrection is the foundation of the Christian faith, and if untrue means our faith is useless—we'll be lost in our sins (15:17). Just as importantly, Paul says Jesus' resurrection is the prototype for our own (15:21–23). A day will come when the One teaching on the mountainside will raise and transform our bodies in the same way his own body will be raised and transformed.

Jesus' resurrection is the foundation of our faith and the blueprint of what lies ahead for us. Miracles like Sean George's give us a taste of that future. When Jesus raises the dead now, he is giving us a glimpse of the day heaven and earth will be made new, and our aching bodies are fully transformed.

That's resilience.

> The Spirit of God, who raised Jesus from the dead, lives in you. And just as God raised Christ Jesus from the dead, he will give life to your mortal bodies by this same Spirit living within you.
>
> ROMANS 8:11

Have you ever doubted Jesus' physical resurrection?

How can our future hope of resurrection affect the way we live now?

TASTING HEAVEN

In Jerusalem, the Lord of Heaven's Armies
will spread a wonderful feast
for all the people of the world.
It will be a delicious banquet
with clear, well-aged wine and choice meat.

ISAIAH 25:6

After releasing the book that told our story, Merryn and I received hundreds of emails from readers. Most were from people telling us the book had helped them start again after their own broken dreams. But to our surprise, one was from a TV producer. And before long a film crew was heading to Oxford to make a documentary on us.[57]

The weeks leading up to filming were intense. There was so much to prepare as we helped producers choose locations, caterers, and clothes. We even found a tandem bicycle for the production!

Of the two of us, Merryn has been the more private, and the thought of describing our journey to a camera made her understandably anxious. We also felt a little vulnerable entrusting our story to someone else's care. Would we like what we saw?

But after all the filming and editing was done, the documentary turned out beautifully—particularly the closing scene, which centers on a dinner party. You see a silky tablecloth drop gently onto our table. You see cutlery set at each place. You see delicious food, and glasses being filled. You see the guests arrive, and people laughing. You see that life can be good even after a broken dream.

Jesus' Sermon is practical, earthy—grounded in the real-world challenges of this life. But it never loses sight of the future. Jesus points to a day when rewards will be given in heaven (Matthew 5:12; 6:20), and a delightful feature of that event will be its culmination in a great banquet of the finest foods and wines (Isaiah 25:6, Revelation 19:6–7). This coming banquet will be on Jesus' mind when he attends a dinner party himself—and must remind his hosts of the unexpected people invited to God's feast (Luke 14:15–24). Then, the night before his death, Jesus will transform the Passover meal into something that points toward that future feast too (Matthew 26:29).

That means every time we share the bread and wine of the Lord's Supper we get a glimpse of the great banquet. But not only that, I believe *every* meal or dinner party we enjoy can become a taste of what's to come. As we lay the tablecloth and set the cutlery, we remember a place is being prepared for us at God's banquet. As dishes are passed and glasses are filled, we catch the aroma of those future delicacies. And as our guests arrive and the laughter begins, we can start sensing this: that one day, all the stress and tears and broken dreams of our lives will be over.

One day, we will take our seat at a table full of joy.

"For the time has come for the wedding feast of the Lamb,
and his bride has prepared herself."

REVELATION 19:7

How could you make meal times a daily taste of heaven?

How can you echo the great banquet by making your dinner parties diverse in guests (Luke 14:12–14)?

PRACTICING RESURRECTION

My dear brothers and sisters, be strong and immovable. Always work enthusiastically for the Lord, for you know that nothing you do for the Lord is ever useless.

1 CORINTHIANS 15:58

So, followers of Jesus look forward to two great events: our personal resurrection to new life, and the "resurrection" of our groaning planet into a new world of peace, beauty, justice, and joy. But while both take place in the future, Jesus says these events are to shape our praying and working *now*, as God's kingdom comes to earth as it is in heaven. Our future hope shapes our present work.

We can take inspiration from groups like the Simple Way community in Philadelphia, Pennsylvania. A few years ago Shane Claiborne and his friends moved into the city's Kensington district where poverty and crime are plentiful. And there, to use poet Wendell Berry's beautiful phrase, they began "practicing resurrection." They've taken abandoned buildings and turned them into community centers where at-risk kids can get help with homework. They've taken overgrown lots and turned them into urban gardens, planting flowers in old TV sets and computer monitors. They've painted colorful murals on the depressing walls of old tenement blocks. They've run street parties with jugglers and artists, handing out school supplies and sharing about Jesus. They've marched for peace, campaigned for justice, and slept on the streets with the homeless. When a child mentioned it was easier to get a gun in their neighborhood than a salad, the Simple Way folks built a greenhouse to grow vegetables to share. The community has gone about "making ugly things beautiful and bringing dead things to life."[58] Following the Sermon on the Mount and inspired by a vision of heaven, they are giving their community a glimpse of God's new world.

Over the years, the Sermon on the Mount has been interpreted in different ways. Some have found its ethics so demanding they've felt it can only apply to a future age, not today. Or that its main purpose is to convict us of sin and our need of salvation, not to guide our lives now. But Jesus doesn't let us off that easily. He says we're to act on everything he's said. Heaven may be on its way, but this life matters too.

The apostle Paul understood this. After talking at length about resurrection—how it will happen and what our new bodies will be like—he ends with a call to action: we are to work "enthusiastically for the Lord," knowing that "nothing you do for the Lord is ever useless" (1 Corinthians 15:58). Our work will not be wasted when judgment day comes and life is transformed. What is begun now will be perfected then.

Future hope motivates present action.

Our job now is to practice resurrection.

So we keep on praying for you, asking our God to enable you to live a life worthy of his call. May he give you the power to accomplish all the good things your faith prompts you to do.

2 THESSALONIANS 1:11

What gifts, talents, and practical abilities do you have? How can you use them to "practice resurrection" in your community?

EMBRACING PAIN

"And a sword will pierce your very soul."

LUKE 2:35

The Mount Grace Priory in North Yorkshire is one of England's best preserved medieval monasteries. For hundreds of years Carthusian monks lived there in solitude, devoting themselves to prayer. The priory's ruins are impressive, but when I visited it was a more recent monument that caught my attention.

Within the church at the center of the priory stands a sculpture called *The Madonna of the Cross*. Crafted by artist Malcolm Brocklesby, it depicts Jesus' mother, Mary, lifting her newborn son to heaven. "Blessed are those who mourn," Jesus has said in his Sermon, and if there was ever a person who would mourn, it would be his own mother. There are many striking aspects to the sculpture, like Mary's posture (determined rather than distraught), and her expression (serene rather than anguished). But perhaps the most striking is that she stands in the form of a cross. As Brocklesby notes in an inscription, Mary knows the suffering inherent in her calling as well as her son's. The cross will be an inescapable part of her existence.

Mary knew early on that her task of parenting the Messiah would be painful. As Simeon told her, "a sword will pierce your very soul" (Luke 2:35). That prophecy was certainly fulfilled at Jesus' crucifixion. Mary stands looking at her son, now lifted up on a bloody, splintery cross (John 19:25). He is suffering. He is innocent. She loves him beyond words. Even now he's concerned for her well-being, putting her into John's care. A sword pierces Mary's soul as a sword pierces her son's side.

There is a cost to each of our callings. An actress I know loses film opportunities because her faith compels her to refuse explicit scenes. C. S. Lewis was never awarded a professorship at Oxford University because of his Christian writings. William Wilberforce probably missed out on becoming British prime minister by resisting the slave trade. Florence Nightingale faced years of opposition from her upper class family who felt disgust at her pursuing the "common" work of nursing. And the apostle Paul was whipped, beaten, stoned, imprisoned, shipwrecked, hunted, and left hungry and cold as he followed his calling (2 Corinthians 11:23–27). Jesus says there's a cost to following him, a cross for us to carry too (Luke 14:26–33).

But there's a reason why Brocklesby's sculpture has Mary looking serene rather than anxious. "She is looking beyond Calvary to the resurrection," he says. Despite the cost, none of those mentioned above would have had it any other way. They went on a daring, risky, redemptive adventure with God, an adventure of eternal significance.

And so, as I reflect on Brocklesby's sculpture, I ask myself: Will I, like Mary, accept the suffering inherent in my own calling? Will I, like her, look beyond the cross to the resurrection? Will I embrace the pain that's necessary to fulfill my assignment? Will I too look beyond it to the victory?

These are the characteristics of the resilient life.

So never be ashamed to tell others about our Lord. And don't be ashamed of me, either, even though I'm in prison for him. With the strength God gives you, be ready to suffer with me for the sake of the Good News.

2 TIMOTHY 1:8

How do you stay encouraged when following Jesus gets difficult? Can you say today, "I will suffer for him" too?

FACING REALITY

"Do you think those Galileans were worse sinners than all the other people from Galilee?" Jesus asked. "Is that why they suffered?"

LUKE 13:2

I met Mike at a conference. As we chatted I noticed a large reddish blemish on his right temple, which he later explained was skin cancer. Mike had suffered through two operations to remove it, but both had failed. So he told me he'd been all ears when a lady had approached him at church saying God had told her why the cancer hadn't been healed yet.

"God says it's one of three things," she told him.

One of three? Mike thought. *You mean, even God doesn't know for sure?*

"It's either a generational curse passed down from your parents . . ."

My skin cancer is my parent's fault?

"Or it's a secret sin in your life . . ."

Which one? (Mike can be cheeky.)

"Or you lack the faith to be healed."

It's natural to look for reasons why you or other people suffer. Resilience researchers say humans recover better when they can make some sense of their pain. But we should beware of simplistic or over-spiritualized answers to pain and its causes. As we've seen, Jesus was reluctant to give blanket answers to human suffering.

Jesus acknowledges that sin can bring illness (Matthew 9:1–8), but when he's asked about the man born blind, Jesus says the condition has nothing to do with sins of the man or his parents. When he's told about some Galileans murdered by Pilate, Jesus says they were no more sinful than anyone else—and neither were the victims of a recent tower collapse in Siloam (Luke 13:1–5). And while faith plays a role in healing (Mark 9:14–29), it isn't a magic formula. We find faithful believers like Paul, Timothy, and Trophimus sick in the Bible.

So what can we say about suffering that will help us make some sense of it? One thing is to understand suffering within the grand four-act drama of history:

Act 1: God creates a world of peace and beauty (Genesis 1–2)

Act 2: The fall of humanity brings evil and suffering into the world (Genesis 3)

Act 3: God starts to fix the world through the nation of Israel, through Jesus' life, death, and resurrection, and now through his church (2 Corinthians 5:18–21)

Act 4: One day he will complete the task, eradicating all death, sorrow, and pain forever (Revelation 21–22)

We are in the middle of Act 3 now, and not yet in Act 4. As Jesus does his work, miracles like Sean George's will happen—but we won't be free of all sorrow and pain until the final scene of this drama comes and a whole new story begins.

"Could there be a fourth possibility for my skin cancer?" Mike asked the woman at his church as their conversation continued.

"What?" she said.

"That I didn't wear my hat enough in the sun when I was younger?"

(I told you he could be cheeky.)

Mike's point is important. In a broken world towers fall, people are born blind, the sun burns hotter than our skin can handle . . . and there may be no other reason than that. This is the reality we must face. We're not in Act 4 yet.

But it's coming.

"He will wipe every tear from their eyes, and there will be no more death or sorrow or crying or pain. All these things are gone forever."

REVELATION 21:4

When calamity strikes, do you assume it's because of someone's sin? Do you ever "over-spiritualize" pain?

VOICING LAMENT

O Lord, how long will you forget me? Forever?
How long will you look the other way?

PSALM 13:1

She sits in sorrow in her room—dark circles under her eyes, tears down her cheeks, a vacant stare on her face. She has worshipped the Almighty since her teenage years but there are unfilled gaps in her life—empty places, hollow spaces, aches and yearnings and unmet longings. And she has prayed, oh how she has prayed, for God to intervene. To give her the desires of her heart, or take them away. One or the other. But she's gotten neither. Just many years of waiting.

Most of us know someone for whom the storms of life have been particularly fierce. Maybe they've lived with chronic pain, faced the loss of a child, had a loved one murdered, or experienced a broken dream—a career gone bad, a marriage that never happened, or some other crushing disappointment. Perhaps you've faced this too. If so, you know it can be cold comfort to be told that suffering is a reality to be faced, that God can turn it into service, that our pain can become strength and our weakness power. In our most anguished moments we want the all-powerful God to intervene *now*. And sometimes he doesn't. That can leave us feeling sad, lonely, weak, even angry.

It astounds me that these very feelings are validated in scripture. Almost half the book of Psalms is made up of what are called "psalms of lament": cries of protest, despair, doubt, complaint. "How long, O Lord, will you look on and do nothing?" David says when under attack (Psalm 35:17). "All night long I prayed," Asaph says, "but my soul was not comforted" (77:2). "Remember how short my life is," cries Ethan, "how empty and futile this human existence!" (89:47). "I am sick at heart," David says during serious illness. "How long, O Lord, until you restore me?" (6:3). As the Spirit was inspiring the biblical writers, he felt no compulsion to leave out these raw emotions—even when they were directed at God. In scripture, disappointment and frustration link arms with praise and adoration. It's impressive that God gives us the best arguments against himself.

Lament is about being honest with God. Not arrogant, not demanding, but honest. Sometimes life stinks. You may feel God has let you down. Voice your lament.

This can make some of us uncomfortable. Aren't we supposed to be respectful to God? Always. Aren't we supposed to trust him in all things? Yes. But we can still be honest with him over our long-term pain. Psalm 13 is a helpful guide in this. David begins the psalm in despair, saying, "O LORD, how long will you forget me?" (13:1). He ends it in hope, saying, "I trust in your unfailing love" (13:5). But his affirmation comes only after he expresses anguish, sorrow, and frustration along the way (13:2–4).

The storms of life will come. During these dark, wintry nights of difficulty, we can voice our lament. The Sermon-giver does. "My God, my God, why have you abandoned me?" Jesus cries, uttering a psalm of lament on the cross (Psalm 22:1; Matthew 27:46).

Our girl still sits in her room. There she is with her heavy heart and mascara-streaked face. How will we help her? By telling her to cheer up because it can't be that bad? By telling her to quit worrying and trust in God? By doing what Job's friends did, trying to theologize the cause of her problems?

Instead, how about sitting with her quietly as she sobs?

And helping her offer her sadness to God.

O LORD, come back to us!
How long will you delay?

PSALM 90:13

How comfortable are you being completely honest with God?

Can you let others grieve without trying to explain or solve their problem?

SEEING GOD

"Dear woman, why are you crying?" Jesus asked her.
"Who are you looking for?"

JOHN 20:15

It was late when the phone rang. The call was from a friend of ours who was getting married in a few months' time. Just a week earlier we'd joined Narelle and her fiancé, Daniel, for the engagement party. There'd been lots of food and laughter and happiness for them, and Narelle's table had overflowed with presents. But I could soon tell she wasn't happy tonight.

"Dan's broken off the engagement," she said, before bursting into tears.

Merryn and I drove round to be with her. Narelle was feeling confused, of course. And rejected. Soon she'd face the humiliating task of handing presents back to each person and explaining why. What's more, some years earlier a previous fiancé had broken an engagement in much the same way. Narelle was in a dark place.

We're told that darkness covered the land during Jesus' crucifixion (Mark 15:33). That darkness hovers over many hearts in the days that follow. It hovers over Mary Magdalene as she stands before a cold, empty tomb on Easter Sunday (John 20:1–11). She's weak from grief. The horror of seeing her beloved, innocent friend killed is made worse by the fact that it seems Jesus' body has been stolen from the grave.

Darkness hovers over Cleopas as he walks along the Emmaus road (Luke 24:13–32). He's confused. The One he believed would liberate the Jews from their enemies has been crucified. That wasn't how things were supposed to end.

Darkness hovers over Peter as he heads back to his old fishing job (John 21:1–3). He's bewildered by everything that's happened and he's feeling ashamed. He said he'd follow Jesus to the end but wound up denying him three times (18:17; 25–27).

And darkness hovers over Thomas as he sits with the disciples, full of doubts and questions (20:24–25). All this strange talk about Jesus having been seen again . . .

Mary, Cleopas, Peter, Thomas—each one of them is in darkness.

And that's where Jesus meets them.

Soon Mary is approached by an enigmatic figure who turns out to be Jesus in disguise (John 20:12–16). Soon Cleopas has his eyes opened to see it's his resurrected Lord who's been walking beside him (Luke 24:30–32). Soon Peter sees Jesus and has his shame removed (John 21:7; 15–19). And soon Thomas sees Jesus and has his doubts answered (20:26–28).

It's a paradox. During life's dark moments, we often question God's goodness or lament his supposed absence. But for many throughout history, it's been during such dark times that God was more profoundly known.

A few weeks after the broken engagement, Merryn and I were in a Bible study with Narelle and some others. At the end of the night I asked for prayer points. Narelle began to cry. I assumed I knew why, but I was wrong.

"I don't want to ask God for anything," she said. "I want to thank him. I've been through some dark times recently, but I've never felt God so close to me as I have these last few weeks." And then she wept more tears—of gratefulness.

Blessed are those who mourn, for they will be comforted.

I had only heard about you before, but now
I have seen you with my own eyes.

JOB 42:5

How have you ever experienced God's closeness through a dark time?
How can you be God's voice and hands to someone in hardship?

LEAVING A LEGACY

"This is not a reference to David, for after David had done the will of God in his own generation, he died and was buried with his ancestors, and his body decayed."

ACTS 13:36

In Britain the residences of famous people are often commemorated with a small blue plaque. The homes of Mozart, Charles Dickens, and Jane Austen are marked like this, as is the Liverpool house where John Lennon once lived. One sign on a famous house here in Oxford reads: *C. S. Lewis, Scholar and Author, lived here 1930–1963.* Many contemporary writers, scientists, politicians, and artists dream of one day having a blue plaque to be remembered by.

Humans throughout history have tried numerous ways to ensure their posterity. Ancient rulers erected palaces, statues, triumphal arches, and other monuments to their glory. Others had their portraits painted, or they published their memoirs. Monarchs prayed for a son to perpetuate the family name. And this drive for posterity isn't limited to the powerful. Deep down, all of us hope our lives and achievements will live on after us. Oh to have a legacy like C. S. Lewis! As a writer, I'd love my books to be read by future generations.

I have a hunch this drive for posterity is part of the longing each of us has for eternity (Ecclesiastes 3:11). We want to live beyond our earthly lives. But the drive has an obvious downside. We can seek our own glory rather than God's, and by trying to be known by future generations we can miss serving our own. The apostle Paul put King David's life into perspective by saying, "After David had done the will of God in his own generation, he died" (Acts 13:36). Paul's main point is that Jesus, not David, is the ultimate King (13:34–37). But along the way Paul said something powerful to us: David's focus was doing God's will for his *own* generation. Any legacy beyond that was up to God.

Statues of Lenin, Stalin, and Hussein have toppled, and more monuments of pride will fall in the future. As scholars tell us, the storms Jesus talks about in his Sermon include not just the trials of life but ultimate judgment too (Matthew 25:31–46). One day Jesus will return, cleanse the world of evil, and require us all to give an account of our lives (Romans 14:10–12). The proud will be removed, hypocrites unmasked, false prophets revealed, all fates sealed. Followers of Jesus will be resilient through this because he took care of our sins at the cross (Romans 3:21–25; 8:1). But on judgment day he wants to see more than a commemorative plaque as our achievement. Everything we've done will be sifted (1 Corinthians 3:13–15). Only deeds of love will last. We'll be rewarded for living the way he's asked.

I'd love my books to span generations the way C. S. Lewis's have. But even if I had half of his talent, that decision would be out of my control. Instead, I'm called to put Jesus' Sermon into action by serving *this* generation with all the gifts, abilities, and love I have. Any legacy beyond that is up to him. And that is actually quite freeing.

For God is not unjust. He will not forget how hard you have worked for him and how you have shown your love to him by caring for other believers, as you still do.

HEBREWS 6:10

How are you looking to leave a legacy?
How can you serve this generation best?

A GOD OF SURPRISES

When Jesus had finished saying these things, the crowds were amazed at his teaching, for he taught with real authority—quite unlike their teachers of religious law.

MATTHEW 7:28–29

Sometimes I wonder what it was like just before creation sprang into existence. Were the angels surprised when God sketched out plans for a universe he didn't need? They must have been—as surprised as when they saw the first waters rush forth and the mountains burst up through the seas. As surprised as when they watched the first bird take flight and saw the first humans open their eyes.

God surprised Abraham with a promise, Sarah with a child, and Moses with a flaming bush that never burned up. All Israel walked in wide-eyed wonder as they followed the cloud and the fire, marched beside walls of water, and fled to a new land.

God surprised Isaac with a wife and Jacob with a dream. He surprised Samuel with a voice and Elijah with a whisper. God surprised David with kingship, Solomon with wisdom, Hezekiah with life, and Isaiah with a vision. And then one day God surprised a teenage girl with an angelic visitation.

The child born to that girl surprised the learned with his knowledge of God. After coming of age and learning a trade, he surprised those around him by setting off on a mission. On that mission he surprised blind men by opening their eyes and the demon-afflicted by casting their tormentors into swine. He surprised crippled women by straightening their backs and wedding hosts by turning water into wine. He surprised the poor with his attention, children with his affection, the leprous with cleansing, and sinners with restoration. It was a surprise when this Lord returned to life after death and offered to forgive the very ones who betrayed him.

And as he's sat on the mountain delivering his Sermon, he's surprised all who've listened (Matthew 7:28–29). He's blessed the poor and troubled, not the rich and well, and said such little people will change the world. He's said conflicts are resolved by loving one's opponents, by turning cheeks and going the extra mile. He's rewritten the rules on living with others, equating anger with murder and overturning customs on vows. He's told us the birds of the air can teach us about trust, and our best desires can help us make choices. He's said weakness can become strength and suffering can become service . . . that a resilient life is made by putting his words into practice.

Putting *his* words into practice. That's been the most surprising thing—the startling weightiness of Jesus' words. He hasn't spoken like other rabbis with their borrowed authority. He hasn't said "the law tells you" or "Moses says." He hasn't even spoken like a prophet, adding "thus says the LORD" to his pronouncements. He's been more audacious than that. Without caution or apology he's said "*I* tell you," "*My* words," and "*I* say" throughout his Sermon. Each of his words has echoed with divine authority.

And now, what surprises await *us* as we take up his challenge? As we accept his invitation to be forgiven, restored, embraced, and rewarded? As we take up our calling to be salt, light, and love in the world? As we develop holy hearts and words, holy commitments and promises, as we give, pray, and trust the way he's shown? As his book, his voice, and his Spirit guide us? As we turn his words into deeds with all the strength we have and practice resurrection with all the creativity we can muster? Here lies the promise as we go forth in our lives with this God of surprises:

At the end of our days we will finish strong, having found the resilience of a Jesus-shaped life.

And we will enjoy his ongoing surprises forever.

And they will reign forever and ever.

REVELATION 22:5

If you were to write your life into a short story, what would it say?

From today, how will you live differently after journeying through Jesus' Sermon?

What surprises await us as we take up his

CHALLENGE? As we take up our calling to be

SALT, LIGHT, and LOVE in the world?

As we develop *holy hearts* and words,

holy commitments and promises? As we

TURN HIS WORDS INTO DEEDS with all the

strength we have and practice resurrection with

all the creativity we can muster?

NOTES

1. Dallas Willard, *The Divine Conspiracy: Rediscovering Our Hidden Life in God* (London, Fount, 1998) page 17.
2. See Dallas Willard, *The Divine Conspiracy* chapter 4; Scot McKnight, *The Story of God Bible Commentary: Sermon on the Mount* (Grand Rapids, Zondervan, 2013) pages 32–38.
3. I am persuaded by scholars like Kenneth Bailey that Jesus was not born in a stable, as popularly thought. Rather, the "inn" mentioned in the story was a guest room in a family home into which animals were often brought to sleep at night. For a helpful explanation read: http://www.biblearchaeology.org/post/2008/11/08/the-manger-and-the-inn.aspx#Article (accessed 5 May 2015).
4. Dallas Willard, *The Divine Conspiracy*, page 17.
5. For example, one Google AdWords search on the phrase "Meaning of life" showed around 500,000 searches a month. https://adwords.google.com (accessed 5 January 2012). And for the record, I don't think these searchers are all looking for the Monty Python skit of the same name.
6. I'm grateful to Richard Foster and Kathryn A. Helmers for this insight, explored in *Life with God: Reading the Bible for Spiritual Transformation* (San Francisco, Harper One, 2008) page ix.
7. This is New Testament scholar Scot McKnight's distillation of what Jesus meant by "blessed" in the Beatitudes. *The Story of God Bible Commentary: Sermon on the Mount*, page 36.
8. Tom Wright, *Simply Jesus: Who He Was, What He Did, Why It Matters* (London, SPCK, 2011) page 216.
9. Some of the cities included in the "Decapolis" region, mostly of Gentile population and culture.
10. John Stott, *The Message of the Sermon on the Mount* (Leicester, IVP, 1992) page 67.
11. Quoted in Chuck Colson and Ellen Santilli Vaughn, *The Body* (Texas, Word, 1992) page 279.
12. "God-flavors" and "God-colors" are Eugene Petersen's lovely phrases for Matthew 5:13–14 in *The Message* (Colorado Springs, NavPress Publishing Group, 2002).
13. This story was recounted to me during a radio interview with Andraé Crouch in May 2001.
14. They're listed in Romans 12:4–8, 1 Corinthians 12:12–31, and Ephesians 4:7–13 and summarized in 1 Peter 4:10–11.
15. Bede recounts Caedmon's story in the fourth book of his *Ecclesiastical History of England*, completed around AD 731 and available online at http://www.ccel.org/ccel/bede/history.html.

16. Oprah interview on *Piers Morgan Tonight*, January 17, 2011, found at http://transcripts.cnn.com/TRANSCRIPTS/1101/17/pmt.01.html.
17. For examples on the theme, see http://en.wikipedia.org/wiki/Oprah_Winfrey#Spiritual_leadership (accessed January 2015).
18. Henri J. M. Nouwen, *Clowning in Rome: Reflections on Solitude, Celibacy, Prayer, and Contemplation* (Garden City, Image Books, 2000) page 9.
19. Francois and Epiphanie's story is told in "Portraits of Reconciliation: 20 years after the genocide in Rwanda, reconciliation still happens one encounter at a time" by photographer Pieter Hugo and Susan Dominus, *The New York Times Magazine*, April 6, 2014, found at www.nytimes.com/interactive/2014/04/06/magazine/06-pieter-hugo-rwanda-portraits.html (accessed November 20, 2014).
20. Professor John Cacioppo, University of Chicago, quoted in Eric Jaffe, "Isolating the Costs of Loneliness," *Observer* magazine, volume 21, number 11, December 2008, found at http://www.psychologicalscience.org/index.php/publications/observer/2008/december-08/isolating-the-costs-of-loneliness.html (accessed November 24, 2014).
21. C. S. Lewis, *The Great Divorce: A Dream* (London, Harper Collins Signature Classic Edition, 2002) chapter 2.
22. For the effects of pornography on individuals and society, see Melinda Tankard Reist and Abigail Bray (editors), *Big Porn Inc.: Exposing the Harms of the Global Pornography Industry* (North Melbourne, Spinifex Press, 2012).
23. For online help, visit www.xxxchurch.com. For software, visit www.x3watch.com.
24. While it was less common, women could instigate divorces by this time too, although it was much more difficult. See Scot McKnight, *The Story of God Bible Commentary: Sermon on the Mount* (Grand Rapids, Zondervan, 2013) pages 98–99.
25. Julia M. O'Brien (editor), *The Oxford Encyclopedia of the Bible and Gender Studies* (Oxford, Oxford University Press, 2014) page 223.
26. Henri J. M. Nouwen, *Clowning in Rome: Reflections on Solitude, Celibacy, Prayer, and Contemplation* (Garden City, Image Books, 1979) page 45.
27. Henri J. M. Nouwen, *Clowning in Rome*, page 48.
28. Some scholars question whether "do not resist an evil person" is the best translation of this verse, suggesting "do not retaliate revengefully" is closer to the original Greek. For more on this see Walter Wink, *The Powers That Be: Theology for a New Millennium* (New York, Galilee, 1998) page 98, and Glen H. Stassen, *Living the Sermon on the Mount: A Practical Hope for Grace and Deliverance* (San Francisco, Jossey-Bass, 2006) page 91. Jesus isn't telling us to submit to evil, but to refuse to oppose it on its own terms.
29. For more on this approach to reading Matthew 5:38–41 see Walter Wink, *The Powers That Be*, chapter 5, and Glen H. Stassen, *Living the Sermon on the Mount*, pages 89–98. I am indebted to Australian peace activist Jarrod McKenna for

encouraging me to dig further into these verses and grasp their surprising intent.

30. I tell this story in more detail in *Unseen Footprints: Encountering the Divine Along the Journey of Life* (Oxford, Lion Hudson, 2007) pages 36–38 and 68–71.
31. This story is found in Danusia Stok (editor), *Kieslowski on Kieslowski* (London, Faber and Faber, 1993) page 176.
32. Richard Foster, *Celebration of Discipline: The Path to Spiritual Growth* (San Francisco, Harper & Row, 2002) page 175.
33. Steve Meacham, "Portrait of the artist as a madman," *The Sydney Morning Herald*, August 29, 2002, found at http://www.smh.com.au/articles/2002/08/28/1030508072787.html (accessed May 7, 2015).
34. Os Guinness, *The Call: Finding and Fulfilling the Central Purpose of Your Life* (Nashville, W Publishing Group, 2003) page 73.
35. However, Keillor may have been discussing a need for authors to be so honest, rather than making a personal confession. See his interview with David Heim, "Wobegon Poets: A Prairie Poem Companion," *The Christian Century*, March 22, 2003, found at www.christiancentury.org/article/2003-03/wobegon-poets (accessed July 2005).
36. Kenneth E. Bailey, *Jesus Though Middle Eastern Eyes: Cultural Studies in the Gospels* (Downers Grove, InterVarsity Press, 2008) page 92.
37. Dallas Willard, *The Divine Conspiracy: Rediscovering Our Hidden Life in God* (London, Fount, 1998) page 284.
38. The project became a popular website and book series: http://postsecret.com.
39. See R. T. Kendall, *Total Forgiveness* (Lake Mary, Florida, Charisma House, 2007). You can hear my interview with R. T. at http://sheridanvoysey.com/023-the-seven-signs-of-forgiveness or read the transcript in my book *Open House Volume 2* (Sydney, Strand, 2009).
40. "Mimi" recounted her story when calling my radio show on April 6, 2008.
41. Scot McKnight suggests this line was inspired by 1 Chronicles 29:11–13 and added while early Christians publicly prayed the Lord's Prayer, leading to its later being added to some copies of the New Testament. While they may not be Jesus' original words, their meaning is biblical.
42. For helpful, practical guidance on fasting see chapter 4 of Richard Foster's classic book on spiritual practices, *Celebration of Discipline*.
43. The advertisement was for Levi Strauss jeans. You can view the commercial here: http://theinspirationroom.com/daily/2003/levi-501-jeans-baptised/ (accessed January 2015).
44. These characteristics are summarized from chapter 2 of *The Selfish Capitalist: Origins of Affluenza* (London, Vermilion, 2008).
45. One interpretation is that the "pearls" are the gospel (see Matthew 13:45–46) and the "pigs" are a particularly brutish type of person who, being so aggressive and abusive, are not to be given the message of Jesus. But is anyone good enough to be given the gospel, or anyone bad enough not

to hear it? Another suggestion is that pearls are of no value to pigs, so the gospel should only be given to those who are ready for it. Others note that Jews commonly called Gentiles "pigs" (that is, "unclean"), so Jesus is saying not to preach to the Gentiles until the Jews have heard the gospel first (see Matthew 15:24). All these suggestions are based on the idea that Jesus is talking about preaching here, but this seems strained. He'll prepare his disciples for preaching later (Matthew 10). The immediate context of Matthew 7 is correction, hence the interpretation I've taken here.

46. Os Guinness, *The Call*, page 70.
47. Christine Sine, "What Do I Want to Become?" http://godspace-msa.com/2015/01/29/what-do-i-want-to-become/ (accessed January 2015).
48. You can read a little more of that story in chapter 2 of my book *Resurrection Year: Turning Broken Dreams into New Beginnings* (Nashville, Thomas Nelson, 2013).
49. In the New Testament, Jesus is recorded quoting most from the Psalms (eleven times) and Deuteronomy (ten times). For a short and helpful article see, "Which Old Testament Book Did Jesus Quote Most?" at http://blog.biblia.com/2014/04/which-old-testament-book-did-jesus-quote-most/ (accessed January 2015).
50. Adapted from Adrian Plass and Jeff Lucas, *Seriously Funny 2* (Milton Keynes, Authentic, 2012) pages 149–150.
51. Paulo Coelho, *The Pilgrimage* (London, HarperCollinsPublishers, 2003) pages 62–64.
52. Quoted in Boris Cyrulnik, *Resilience: How Your Inner Strength Can Set You Free from the Past* (London, Penguin, 2009) page 156.
53. Martin E. P. Seligman, "Building Resilience," *Harvard Business Review*, April 2011, available at https://hbr.org/2011/04/building-resilience (accessed February 2015).
54. The book is called *Resurrection Year: Turning Broken Dreams into New Beginnings* (Nashville, Thomas Nelson, 2013).
55. You can read my interview with Nick Vujicic in my book *Open House Volume 3* (Sydney, Strand Publishing, 2010) or listen to it at http://sheridanvoysey.com/003-the-nick-vujicic-interview-podcast/.
56. See Sheridan Voysey, *Open House Volume 3* (Sydney, Strand Publishing, 2010) for the transcript of my interview with Dr. George.
57. The short film is called *A Journey through Broken Dreams* (Day of Discovery TV, 2014).
58. For more see Shane Claiborne, *The Irresistible Revolution: Living as an Ordinary Radical* (Grand Rapids, Zondervan, 2006) pages 121–123 and http://www.huffingtonpost.com/shane-claiborne/practicing-resurrection-t_b_1443621.html (accessed March 2014).

ABOUT THE AUTHOR

Sheridan Voysey is an author, speaker, and broadcaster based in Oxford, United Kingdom. He is the author of eight books, including *The Making of Us, Resurrection Year, Reflect with Sheridan*, and *Unseen Footprints*, and he writes regularly for the *Our Daily Bread* devotional. Sheridan is a presenter of *Pause for Thought* on BBC Radio 2's Breakfast Show; is a regular guest on other broadcast networks across the United States, United Kingdom, Australia, and beyond; and speaks at conferences and events around the world. Sheridan is husband to Merryn and walking buddy to his dog, Rupert.

For articles and videos, and to subscribe to Sheridan's podcast *More Than This*, please visit **www.sheridanvoysey.com**

And join him on social media:

Facebook: www.facebook.com/sheridanvoysey
Twitter: @sheridanvoysey

Help us get the word out!

Our Daily Bread Publishing exists to feed the soul with the Word of God.

If you appreciated this book, please let others know.

- Pick up another copy to give as a gift.
- Share a link to the book or mention it on social media.
- Write a review on your blog, on a bookseller's website, or at our own site (odb.org/store).
- Recommend this book for your church, book club, or small group.

Connect with us:

@ourdailybread

@ourdailybread

@ourdailybread

Our Daily Bread Publishing
PO Box 3566
Grand Rapids, Michigan 49501 USA

books@odb.org